# ANTI INFLAMMATORY + MEDITERRANEAN DIET

# Mixed up IF

## Meal plans &

## +200 recipes cookbook

**PAY ATTENTION PLEASE:**
**THIS IS NOT A MEDICAL BOOK!**

**It only describes a common and typical type of diet.**

**IF YOU SUFFER FROM SERIOUS DISEASES IT'S NOT FOR YOU: CONTACT YOUR DOCTOR AND LISTEN TO HIS ADVICE!**

# TABLE OF CONTENTS

## BOOK 1

# BOOK2

# BOOK 3

# MEDITERRANEAN DIET MEAL PLAN

## *The Secret to the Right Eating Choices and Better Health*

# Chapter 1. What is Mediterranean Diet?

Mediterranean diet is by far the most favorite diet amongst the people. In fact, the Mediterranean diet is ranked as the number 1 diet in _Best Diets Overall_ and _Best Plant-Based Diet._

Mediterranean diet is basically the term coined for the traditional eating habits and patterns of people living in the countries near the Mediterranean Sea. There were around 16 countries that were located near that sea.

Mediterranean diet includes natural and unprocessed food. It has hearty servings of fruits, vegetables, whole grains, seafood, and good fats. Unlike many diets, the Mediterranean diet is rich in flavors.

One can devour a myriad of flavors given by nature and reap plenty of benefits from this diet. The Mediterranean diet has gained immense popularity in today's era. This is because of the excellent health history of the people who resided in the Mediterranean area. Compared to the Americans, the citizens of the countries bordering the Mediterranean Sea lived longer. They were free from dangerous ailments like cancer and cardiovascular illness.

The reason behind their active and healthy lifestyle was their diet. Their diet had minimal sugar, saturated fats, and red meat.

Mediterranean diet doesn't have fixed patterns or hard and fast rules. This is because of the people's diverse cultures and eating habits in the Mediterranean region.

For example, Italians' eating habits and diets differed from the Greeks. Similarly, Spain, France, and Rome had some distinctive eating cultures and traditions.

But the diets of all the Mediterranean countries had some fundamental similarity in their diet, which was:

A considerable portion of fruits, vegetables, grains, nuts, beans, and seeds.
Olive oil was used as a primary source of fat.
Dairy products such as milk, cream, cheese, and yogurt are moderate.
Eggs, fish, and poultry as the protein source.

The best thing about this diet is that it includes all the nutrients. The meals prepared in this diet aren't bland. One can enjoy all the flavors and receive many benefits from this diet, such as:

*   Healthy heart health
*   Normalized blood sugar
*   Weight loss
*   Lower levels of bad cholesterol
*   Prevents and fights off chronic diseases.

# How Does Mediterranean Diet Work?

The Mediterranean diet is basically a plant-based diet plan. It includes regular intake of olive oil, whole grains, fruits, vegetables, nuts, herbs, spices, and dairy products in limited quantities. The diet also includes animal protein in smaller portions. It emphasizes consuming seafood, especially fish, forgetting the protein. The Mediterranean diet gives an overview of a person's foods. However, it does not specify the exact quantity of the food to be taken.

It is up to the dieter to specify the amount of each food he consumes according to his choice, weight, and energy requirement. The notable features of this diet that distinguishes it from other diets are:

## • It Emphasis on Healthy Fats

Many fad diets ask the dieters to stay away from fats or consume them in very little quantity. However, the Mediterranean diet promotes the consumption of healthy fats. It recommends replacing butter and margarine with olive oil.

The Mediterranean diet also recommends the intake of nuts, avocados, and oily fish, which are a rich source of healthy fats.

## • Fish as Protein Source

Fish lovers find this diet the best. Not only do the dieters get to enjoy the delectable taste of fish, but they also get tons of benefits from it.

The Mediterranean diet focuses on fish as the primary source of protein instead of meat or poultry. Fish contains plenty of vitamins and omega 3 fats which are excellent for heart health.

## • Water as a Main Beverage

This is the common characteristic of the Mediterranean diet with other diet and meal plans. Water contains 0 calories. This makes it an ideal choice of beverage to quench the thirst and hydrate the body.

The Mediterranean diet also allows dairy products such as milk as a protein and fat source.

All the food groups included in the Mediterranean diet are natural and unprocessed. These nourish our body with the necessary nutrients, vitamins, and minerals. This, in return, keeps our bodies healthy and active. Apart from this, the Mediterranean diet offers ample benefits for your body.

The next chapter will cover all the benefits of this special diet.

# Chapter 2. Health Benefits of the Mediterranean Diet

The Mediterranean diet is a win-win situation for the dieters. One can tantalize their taste buds with a wide variety of food options and gain the immense benefits provided by this diet. Let's discuss in detail the health benefits of the Mediterranean diet.

## Health Benefits of the Mediterranean Diet

### 1. Promotes Heart Health

Unhealthy fats, junk food, and an inactive lifestyle cause high cholesterol and blood pressure problems as we age.

The fat sticks to the side of the arteries and narrows the space for the blood to pass. The blood has to squeeze in the narrow arteries and circulate in the body. This leads to high blood pressure and rapid heartbeat. In severe cases, high blood pressure can prove fatal for the person. It can result in brain hemorrhage or even death.

Following the Mediterranean diet will lead the person to enjoy healthy and unprocessed foods. It will help him flush the toxins from his body and fuel up with essential nutrients. In return, this will help him lower his blood pressure and keep the heart hale and healthy.

### 2. Normalizes Blood Sugar Levels

We discussed what happens to your body when your blood sugar level increases in the previous chapter.

In the present era, people give less attention to their health. Instead of using health and nutrition, they prefer to taste and ease. Hence, the aisle of frozen foods in the supermarket and drive-thru of fast food chains are never empty.

The more carbs we consume, the more our body metabolizes and converts it into glucose. The increased amount of glucose in the bloodstream affects the organs and the body's healthy functioning.

The Mediterranean diet provides and recommends a balanced diet. It emphasizes eating protein, healthy fats, fiber, minerals, and vitamins. When our diet has fewer carbs, our liver and pancreas rest from producing insulin to allow the glucose to absorb in the cells. This keeps our blood sugar in the normal range and prevents the risk of Type 2 diabetes.

## 3. Protects Brain Functions

Many studies and research show that the Mediterranean diet is helpful to protect brain function and prevent diseases related to it, such as Alzheimer's, Parkinson's, Dementia, and other cognitive impairment.

The rick anti-oxidants present in the Mediterranean diet preserve the cell from undergoing oxidative stress, damaging the brain cells. It slashes down the risk of brain diseases and memory loss problems.

## 4. Prevents Muscle Weakness

Our muscles lose their shape and strength as our age advances. However, following the Mediterranean diet reduces the risk of muscle weakness. The diet plays a significant emphasis on protein from fish. This energizes the muscles and keeps them strong even at old age.

## 5. Aids in Weight Loss

Our body stores the unused energy as fat. Over time, when the fat stored in our body increases, it adds extra pounds to our body.

Increased consumption of junk, fried, and processed food is the main weight gain. And to top it off, the inactive lifestyle makes it hard to use the stored fat as energy.

The Mediterranean diet includes foods that are consumed fresh. For instance, nuts, fruits, vegetables, water, etc. These food items are not processed, and to take the full benefit out of these items, one should prepare the food and eat it right away.

Switching from junk and instant food to freshly prepared food with whole and natural ingredients will make your body maintain the optimum weight. With more protein and fiber in the diet, a person feels full. This suppresses the urge to munch unhealthy snacks, which is very helpful in shedding unhealthy weight.

# Chapter 3. Menopause and the Mediterranean Diet

The Mediterranean diet is also helpful for females over the 40s and 50s. This is the period when menopause occurs, and a woman's body undergoes many changes. These changes impact the woman's physical, emotional, and mental health.

Choosing a Mediterranean diet for making healthy food choices can help the woman curb the effects of menopause.

Before we proceed to discuss how the Mediterranean diet is helpful of menopause, let's see:
- What is menopause?
- Potential Risks connected with Menopause.

## What is Menopause?

Menopause is the time in a woman's life when her monthly menstrual cycle ends. Menopause is diagnosed once a woman aged 40 or more goes without the period for a year. There is no fixed age for menopause. It varies from woman to woman. However, the expected age range is between 40 to 50 years.

In the United States of America, the average age where menopause occurs is 51.

Menopause causes lower energy levels, disturbed sleep, loose skin, anxiety, depression, and obesity. Menopause cannot be reversed. However, its stressful effects can be dealt with proper lifestyle changes, a healthy diet, and physical exercise.

## Potential Risks Connected With Menopause

After a woman is diagnosed with menopause, she is more at risk for the following diseases and medical conditions:

## 1. Slow Metabolism and Obesity

Estrogen is a hormone that controls body weight. After a woman stops receiving her monthly cycle, her estrogen level drops.

The lower levels of estrogen lead to a slower metabolism. The body takes time to convert the food into fuel for bodily functions. Moreover, the body's ability to use stored fat as an energy source also reduces.

This contributes to piling up extra calories to the already stored fat in the body. It becomes difficult for the body to use fat stores for energy. As a result, the body piles up unhealthy pounds of fat.

## 2. Cardiovascular Disease

With slow metabolism and increased fat in the body, the risk of cardiovascular diseases multiplies. The cholesterol level rises in the blood, and it takes place inside the walls of the arteries. This creates difficulty for the blood to pass around. The heart pumps more blood and exerts extra pressure to move the blood in the clogged arteries.
This stress on the heart combined with fat-lined arteries is the culprit for cardiovascular diseases, such as heart attack, emphysema, shortness of breath, etc.

## 3. Osteoporosis

The term osteoporosis means 'porous bone.' In this condition, the bones become weak and lose their strength over time. This condition also increases the risk of fracture because of the low bone density.
Osteoporosis continues to over 2 million fractures each year. This number is escalating with each year.
Osteoporosis is a common condition when people above 50 are more at risk of developing it. According to many studies, women are 4 times more prone to developing this disease than men. Women rapidly lose their bone density during the first few years of menopause. It puts them at a greater risk of osteoporosis.

## 4. Urinary Incontinence

Once women cross 40, their vaginal and urethral tissue weakens. The tissues lose their elasticity, due to which they experience a sudden and strong urge to urinate. In severe cases, there is an involuntary loss of urine while talking, laughing, or lifting weight.
Urine incontinence also contributes to urine infections which can be painful for some women.

## 5. Anxiety and Depression

The low estrogen level, slow metabolism, and inactive lifestyle often affect females' mental health.

They stress about things and experience mild symptoms of anxiety and nervousness. In severe cases, this leads to mild to moderate depression.

## The Mediterranean Diet to Manage Risks Associated With Menopause

The risk associated with menopause worsens and deteriorates women's health in the long term. It also hinders them from leading an active, healthy, and happy life.

But thanks to the Mediterranean diet can reduce the risk of the diseases mentioned above, especially obesity.

The central premise of the Mediterranean diet is the right and healthy food choices to fuel up the body. It focuses on whole grains, seafood, dairy products, nuts, and healthy fats. The foods recommended in the Mediterranean diet fuel up the body with the right ingredients and flush toxins.

The protein from fish and plants is helpful to maintain and strengthen muscles mass. The inclusion of dairy products in the diet puts the risk of osteoporosis at bay. Moreover, nuts and healthy fats benefit heart health, sagging skin, and hair thinning.

The Mediterranean diet doesn't include large portions of carbohydrates. This means our body will switch to burning fats for generating energy to keep moving. This is immensely helpful to shed weight. Another way this diet makes weight loss easier is by emphasizing the regular intake of fiber. The fiber present in fruits, vegetables, beans, nuts, etc., satiates hunger and keeps the person full for a longer time. This, in return, reduces the munching and snacking between the main meals.

# Chapter 4. How to Get Started With the Mediterranean Diet?

To begin with, the Mediterranean diet, make sure that you understand the portion and consumption of the different food groups in your daily diet

| Regular Intake | Moderate Intake | Rarely Eaten |
| --- | --- | --- |
| <ul><li>Fruits</li><li>Vegetables</li><li>Nuts</li><li>Legumes</li><li>Olive oil</li><li>Herbs</li><li>Grains</li><li>Seafood</li></ul> | <ul><li>Chicken</li><li>Eggs</li><li>Cheese</li><li>Milk</li><li>Yogurt</li></ul> | <ul><li>Red meat</li><li>Sugary beverages</li><li>Processed meat</li><li>Refined grains/oils</li><li>Other processed food</li></ul> |

The table above shows the foods that should be consumed regularly, frequently, and rarely. The main principle of this diet is to include plant-based and seafood daily in your diet. Other food items such as dairy products and processed foods can also be enjoyed once in a while. To begin your preparation for the Mediterranean diet, make sure to buy the following ingredients.

## Shopping List to Start the Mediterranean Diet

Stock up your pantry and refrigerator with the following items.

## 1. Fruits

Add as many fruits as you can. You can make a fruit salad for your meals or simply much them during the day.
Fill up your shopping basket with apples, strawberries, oranges, grapes, dates, bananas, and any other fruit that you see.

## 2. Vegetables

You can either prepare your meals with fresh vegetables or use frozen vegetables.
Shop for leafy green vegetables as they are the powerhouse of vitamins and minerals. Also, stock up your refrigerator with carrots, avocados, potatoes, corns, cauliflower, onions, etc. There are no restrictions on fruits and vegetables in the Mediterranean diet.

## 3. Seeds and Nuts

While you are on the Mediterranean diet, you cannot snack on fried or processed food. To keep yourself full, you must snack on healthy items.
Nuts and seeds are the perfect healthy snacks. Hence, don't forget to add them to your cart.
Keep almonds, walnuts, hazelnut, macadamia nuts, cashew, and pistachios within your reach to munch on them.
Similarly, fill up your jars with pumpkin seeds and sunflower seeds.

## 4. Whole Grains

You don't have to make any changes in the grains section. All that you have to do is switch from all-purpose flour to wheat.
Thus, purchase the wheat bread and pasta. Also, add brown rice, rye, barley, and buckwheat.

## 5. Seafood

Shop wholeheartedly for seafood. There are many recipes on the internet that you can use to season and prepare your seafood.
Seafood is the main source of animal protein in the Mediterranean diet. Buy salmon, trout, shrimps, tuna, clams, crabs, and oysters as per your preference.

## 6. Other Items

The first 5 things mentioned in the list should be the first ones to go in your basket. Once you are done shopping for the daily food items, shop for the food that you'll eat in moderation. For example, chicken, turkey, eggs, and dairy products.

## 7. Herbs and Spices

The Mediterranean diet is not a huge fan of salt or other sodium seasonings. Therefore, fill up your spice shakers with basil, mint, rosemary, cinnamon, nutmeg, and pepper.

## 8. Oils and Butters

Use extra virgin olive oil to prepare your meals. You can also opt for avocado oil for healthy fats.
Discontinue the use of butter and margarine and switch to using peanut butter or sunflower seed butter.

Once you've purchased all the items, you are ready to switch to the Mediterranean diet and transform your body.

# Chapter 5. Helpful Tips for Following the Mediterranean Diet

The Mediterranean diet is easy to follow. Unlike intermittent fasting, you don't have to restrict yourself from eating, nor do you have to cut a food group completely from your diet.
Below is the list of helpful tips to make it easier to follow and stick to the Mediterranean diet.

## Top 09 Super Helpful Tips to Follow and Stick to the Mediterranean Diet

### 1. Don't Call It a Diet

It is common for people to feel hungrier or overstuff themselves than usual when they decide to diet.
Ever wondered why does it happen? This is because our brain perceives the word *diet* as punishment. When you think about cutting several foods from your diet altogether, you overthink about it. As a result, you exhaust yourself, and your determination becomes weak.
Hence, to stop this pattern and ace the Mediterranean diet, make sure you cut off the word diet. Instead, think of the Mediterranean diet as a lifestyle change. A change that will lead you to a happy, healthy, and active lifestyle.
So, instead of saying '*I am on a diet*,' say '*I am adopting a healthy lifestyle*.' This simple tip will help you to follow and continue the Mediterranean diet.
Moving on to our second tip, which is…

### 2. Clear the Junk Food Stock

Have you heard the popular saying '*Out of sight, out of mind*'?
People often end up eating junk food not because of hunger but because of its reachability.
If a pack of crisps is closer, a person will eventually open it and start munching. You can enjoy crisps and other processed foods in the Mediterranean diet but not daily.
Hence, to prevent snacking on unhealthy items, clear them from your home. Empty your junk food stash from the pantry and kitchen cabinets. Also, remove the processed meat and frozen items, such as nuggets, burger patties, etc.
Once your house is clear from junk food, you won't snack mindlessly during the day. Clearing junk food will also allow you to make room for healthy snacks.

## 3. Keep Nuts and Seeds within Your Reach

Shop for a variety of nuts and seeds. Don't place them in the top cabinets or in the place where you won't see them, let alone reach them.

Fill up small jars and keep them in the places where you can easily reach for them without having to stand up or open a cabinet or drawer. Place them on your dining table, bedside table, or office table.

Simply open the jar and munch on the healthy nuts when you feel like eating something.

Before buying the nuts, don't forget to read the labels. Reading labels will let you know the amount of sugar and salt present in the food.

## 4. Read Food Labels

The majority of the packages and canned food contain a huge percentage of sodium or sugar. Instead of helping your body shed weight, a high amount of sodium and sugar contributes to weight gain.

Sodium and other preservatives increase water retention in your body, leading to bloating, flatulence, and overall discomfort.

Overload of sugar surpasses the normal range of glucose in the body. It disrupts insulin sensitivity and stores unused energy as a fat reserve.

Thus, be mindful during your grocery shopping. Read the labels and buy items with little to no salt, sugar, or other preservatives.

Moving on to the next tip, which is…

## 5. Plan Your Meals Ahead

People are running around the clock. They have little to no time to prepare meals at home. After a tiring day from work or school, they prefer takeaways or online food delivery.

You can save yourself from ordering junk and processed food by planning and prepping your meals ahead. Plan your meals for at least a week. Once you decide on the menu, start prepping for yourself.

You can chop the vegetables, steam them, and then freeze them to use later. In the same way, you can season your seafood so that on the scheduled day, you just have to bake or grill it.

Another thing that you can do is to cook a large batch and freeze half of it for later use. So, on the days when you have zero energy left to cook your meals, you can enjoy homemade food. All that you'll have to do is toss the batch in the microwave and wait for the timer to go up.

## 6. Don't Starve Yourself

Eating healthy on a Mediterranean diet doesn't mean you have to torture yourself or stay hungry until the next mealtime.

Instead of starving yourself, you can take light and healthy snacks. For example, you can have fresh fruits, salad, or nuts to satiate your midday hunger pangs. If you starve yourself to avoid eating before the meal, it will weaken your determination. You will soon revert to your old lifestyle and eating patterns.

Hence, eat whenever you want to but choose healthy snacks over junk and processed food.

## 7. Swap High sugar and Carb Foods with Healthier Versions

Let's face it…a decadent slice of chocolate cake is more appealing than apple slices. However, there is a huge difference between the calories each food item contains.

Eating a chocolate cake slice might tantalize your taste buds. But imagine the number of calories, sugar, and carbs it contains. So, be smart and fulfill your dessert cravings with a healthier version. For instance, you can enjoy apple and peanut butter as your dessert. Similarly, if you want to have a tangy fizzy drink, you can make lemonade to curb your cravings.

And if you really want to have something, then go ahead and enjoy it. The Mediterranean diet allows the consumption of processed and high sugar food once in a while. However, don't forget you can enjoy it rarely, and not daily.

## 8. Don't Deprive Yourself

Unlike other fad diets, the Mediterranean diet allows the occasional consumption of red and processed meat, junk food, and foods packed with carbs and sugar.

If you are carving to eat something that isn't part of the daily food group, no problem. You can enjoy it. It's okay to treat yourself once in a while. Schedule a day in the month where you allow yourself to enjoy whatever you want. Treating yourself once in a blue moon will help you stay dedicated to the Mediterranean diet.

If you strictly adhere to healthy food and do not allow yourself to eat junk food, you won't stick to this diet for a long time.

## 9. Include Exercise or Workout Plan

Incorporating light exercises or your favorite workout will help you get the most of the Mediterranean diet.

You will see and experience the benefits of the Mediterranean diet sooner with exercise. Try to include a simple activity such as walking or jogging for 30 to 60 minutes.  It will improve your blood circulation, strengthen your muscle, and help you get rid of fat stores in your body.

# Chapter 6. Meal Plan for the Mediterranean Diet

Below we have presented a sample menu for 7 days for the Mediterranean diet.
You can adjust the meals and portions according to your likings. The best part? You can enjoy a healthy serving of snacks between the meals.

| Day | Breakfast | Lunch | Dinner |
|---|---|---|---|
| 1 | omelet with tomatoes and olives | whole-grain tuna sandwich with vegetables | grilled salmon with salad and baked potato wedges |
| 2 | oatmeal with raisins, nuts, and apple slices coated with peanut butter | stuffed zucchini pesto with turkey sausages, tomatoes, bell peppers, and cheese | baked shrimps with brown rice and vegetables |
| 3 | Scrambled eggs and sautéed vegetables with whole wheat toast | a quinoa salad with chickpeas | Mediterranean lasagna with sautéed vegetables |
| 4 | omelet with mushrooms, tomatoes, and onions | Zucchini noodles with mozzarella, cherry tomatoes, extra virgin olive oil, and white vinegar | tuna salad with greens and avocado oil, and a fruit salad with nuts |
| 5 | Greek yogurt with strawberries and flax seeds | falafel bowl with feta, onions, cherry tomatoes, hummus, and brown rice | Mediterranean pizza made with whole wheat pita bread. Topped with cheese, vegetables, and olives |
| 6 | oatmeal with blueberries | a whole grain sandwich with hummus and vegetables | a salad with tomatoes, olives, cucumbers, grilled chicken strips, |

and feta cheese

| 7 | Greek yogurt with sliced fruit and nuts | Whole wheat pasta with bell peppers, cherry tomatoes, pepper, and balsamic vinegar | a tuna salad with leafy green veggies and olive oil |

# Chapter 7. Mediterranean Ketogenic Diet

We've discussed what the Mediterranean diet is, what its potential benefits are, and how one can onboard this diet.

Similarly, in the previous section of intermittent fasting, we study the famous keto diet, its benefits, and following it.

Both the Mediterranean and Ketogenic have many benefits stirred for the people. It shed weight, flushes toxins, regulates sugar and insulin level, and keeps many fatal diseases at bay. Mediterranean Keto diet is a new diet that combines the goodness of both diets into one. Following the Mediterranean keto diet provides the combined benefits of the keto and Mediterranean diet.

So, we can say the Mediterranean keto diet includes keto-friendly foods found in the popular Mediterranean diet and creating an eating plan that contains keto low-carb, high amount of good fats, and macronutrients.

Let's discuss the characteristics of this diet plan.

# Key Characteristics of the Mediterranean Keto Diet

## 1. Restricted Carbs to Induce Ketosis

The net carb consumption should be under 25 grams to make the body switch from glucose to fat stores for energy. Once ketosis is induced, the body relies on the stored fat to produce fuel and keep it moving.

Carb restriction and ketosis help reduce weight, regulate insulin levels, normalize blood sugar, and lower the body's bad cholesterol level.

## 2. Increased Intake of Monounsaturated and Polyunsaturated Fats

Eating good fats and protein is the basic principle of the keto diet. The Mediterranean diet also promotes good fats to reduce the bad cholesterol and promote good cholesterol in the blood. This diet includes a hearty portion of olive oil, avocados, fatty fish, nuts, and seeds to fill the body with good fats, protein, and vitamins.

## 3. Getting Carbs from Keto-Friendly Vegetables

The inclusion of vegetables, especially the leafy green ones, is a must in the Mediterranean keto diet. But some vegetables contain high content of carbs. Hence, make sure to limit the intake of those vegetables in your daily diet. Eat them in moderation so that the carbs present in the vegetables don't surpass the daily requirement.

## 4. Daily Protein Intake

Protein is an important nutrient for dieters. It keeps them full, builds muscles, and curbs hunger. The main sources of getting protein in this diet are similar to the Mediterranean diet. Use seafood, especially fatty fish, to get your proteins. To get your daily protein requirement, you can also include chicken, lamb, turkey, eggs, and lentils.
The Mediterranean diet doesn't include red meat or processed meat as a part of the daily diet. The same rule applies to the Mediterranean keto diet.

## 5. Adjust Protein and Fat Portion Based on Your Goals

The 2 main nutrients of this diet are fats and proteins. Adjust the portion size and serving of each nutrient according to your goals.
For example, if your goal is to shed weight, you can decrease the protein portion and add more fats to your diet. As it will accelerate ketosis, which helps you burn more fats.
On the other hand, if your goal is to get leaner and build muscle mass, you should aim for a larger portion of proteins and lesser fats and carbs.

# Chapter 8.  Studies and Researches on the Mediterranean Keto Diet

The Mediterranean and Keto Diet is not an overnight invention or a trending diet on the internet.
This diet is proper research and backed by science. Below are some of the studies that highlight the benefits of this special diet.
Let's have a look at them.


## Research No. 1

In 2008, Spanish researchers designed a Mediterranean keto diet plan for 3 months for 22 obese men. Here are some key features of their diet plan:

1.  No calorie restriction

2.  Olive oil was used as a major fat source. The participants were given the above 2 tablespoons on a daily basis.

3.  Green vegetables as a carb source.

4.  Fish as the primary protein source.

5.  Participants were also allowed to consume a moderate amount of wine, i.e., 200-400 ml/day.

The participants had a high-fat percentage in their bodies. Some of them also had blood pressure, high levels of bad cholesterol, diabetes, and slow metabolism
After the 3 months, the researchers concluded the following results:

• The majority of the participants had lost a significant amount of weight, as much as 30 pounds.

• At the start of the study, 22 men had metabolic syndrome. After three months of the Mediterranean keto diet, they fully recovered from this syndrome.

- Participants had trimmed their waistlines. Many of them had lost up to 16 inches.

- Researchers also observed a shift in BMI. At the beginning of the diet, the average BMI of men was 37. It later changed to 31.5 because of the body fat that participants lost after the diet.

- The blood sugar level of the participants was also improved. It dropped from 118 to the normal range.

- The good cholesterol level increased up to 58.

- Triglycerides dropped to 109, signaling better heart health.

- The participants who were *'pre-hypertensive' went* to *'normotensive.'*

- Researchers also found a reduction in liver fat. Some of the participants who had liver-related diseases were free of them after the 3 months diet.

The results made it clear that the Mediterranean keto diet is ideal for people who want to reduce their weight, improve their heart health, and wave goodbye to chronic diseases like diabetes, cholesterol, and blood pressure.

Let's move on to the next research…

# Research No. 2

A few years later, the same group of Spanish researchers conducted another study. This time they kept the timeframe of 6 weeks. They used the same diet plan and also included some herbal extracts in the plan.

The following were the results after 6 weeks:

- Subjects had a lower level of LDL cholesterol. At the beginning of the study, their average LDL level was 150 mg/ dl. After six weeks, it lowered down to 136 mg/dl.

- The HDL cholesterol levels increased from 46 mg/dl to 52 mg/dl.

# Research No. 3

Another study was conducted in 2015. The participants of this study had higher fat levels, increased glucose, and triglycerides. Moreover, the participants had greater inflammation levels.

At the end of the diet, the result was the same as the previous two studies. The participants shed weight, but their glucose, blood pressure, cholesterol levels were also normalized.

Many other studies show similar results to the ones stated above. The Mediterranean keto diet is backed by proper research and studies. Hence, you can confidently onboard this diet and witness the miraculous transformation of your body by yourself.

dark chocolate                    salad                    Mediterranean salsa

# Mediterranean Diet Breakfast Recipes

# Mediterranean Diet Breakfast Recipes

# 1. Pumpkin Parfait

**Preparation time:** 05 minutes
**Cooking time:** 0 minutes
**Servings:** 3

## Ingredients

- 2 cups homemade pumpkin purée
- ¾ cup Greek yogurt
- 2 tablespoons mascarpone cheese
- ½ tablespoon vanilla extract
- 1 ¼ tablespoon brown sugar
- ¾ teaspoon ground cinnamon
- ¼ teaspoon nutmeg
- 1 tablespoon honey
- Chocolate chips, walnuts, and hazelnuts for garnishing

## Directions

1. Take a large mixing bowl and add all the ingredients except chocolate chips, walnuts, and hazelnuts. Take an electric mixer to combine all the ingredients until it the texture becomes smooth.
2. Transfer the mixture into a serving bowl. Refrigerate the pumpkin-yogurt mixture for 30 minutes.
3. Garnish with chocolate chips, walnuts, and hazelnuts before serving.

## Nutrition

- Calories: 71.7
- Fat: 2.05 g.
- Carbohydrates: 9.75 g.
- Protein: 6.1 g.
- Fiber: 2.5 g.
- Calcium: 47.6 mg

# 2. Mediterranean Vegetable Frittata Recipe

**Preparation time:** 15 minutes
**Cooking time:** 30 minutes
**Servings:** 2

## Ingredients
- ½ red bell pepper chopped
- ½ small zucchini chopped
- Salt and black pepper to taste
- 1 green onion chopped
- 1 oz. broccoli cut into small florets
- ¾ tablespoon extra-virgin olive oil
- 2 medium-sized eggs
- $^{1/8}$ cup milk
- ¼ cup feta cheese
- ¼ teaspoon fresh thyme
- 2 tablespoon parsley chopped

## Directions
1. Preheat the oven to $450^0$ F and set the middle rack of the oven. Place a pan with a rimmed sheet in the oven and let it heat.
2. Take a mixing bowl and add all the vegetables (*except parsley*), olive oil, salt, and pepper. Mix it nicely to coat the veggies in oil and seasonings.
3. Remove the pan from the oven and spread the vegetables over it. Put it back into the oven for 15 minutes at 400° F or until the veggies are soft
4. Take another bowl and whisk together eggs and all the remaining ingredients. Add the baked vegetables and mix again.
5. Add ¼ tsp olive oil to an oven-safe pan. Pour the egg mixture and let it cook for 3-4.
6. Once the bottom of the eggs is set, transfer the pan to the oven for 10 to 12 minutes.
7. Generously sprinkle feta cheese and parsley before serving.

## Nutrition
- Calories: 34.075
- Carbohydrates: 1.2 g.
- Fats: 2.55 g.
- Protein: 1.95 g.

- Fiber: 0.275 g.

# 3. Creamy Tahini Banana Date Shake

**Preparation time:** 5 minutes
**Cooking time:** 0 minutes
**Servings:** 3

## Ingredients
- 2 bananas sliced
- 4 dates
- ¼ cup tahini
- ½ cup crushed
- 1 ½ cups unsweetened almond milk
- 1/4 tsp ground cinnamon

## Directions
1. Add all the ingredients to the blender except for cinnamon. Blend until the shake is creamy and smooth.
2. Pour the shake into serving cups. Sprinkle ground cinnamon and serve.

## Nutrition
- Calories: 299
- Carbohydrates: 47.7 g.
- Fats: 12.4 g.
- Protein:  5.7 g.
- Fiber: 5.6 g

# 4. Mediterranean Breakfast Toast

**Preparation time:** 10 minutes
**Cooking time:** 0 minutes
**Servings:** 2

## Ingredients
- 2 thick slices of whole-grain bread
- ½ cup of hummus
- Pinch of Kosher salt and black pepper
- 1 cucumber sliced into circles
- 2 medium tomatoes, sliced
- 2 tablespoon olives, finely chopped
- Crumbled feta cheese
- Handful baby arugula

## Directions
1. Toast the slices of bread as per your liking.
2. Spread hummus on each bread slice. Sprinkle salt and pepper and top it with the remaining ingredients.

## Nutrition
- Calories: 200
- Carbohydrates: 18.7 g.
- Fats: 11.3 g.
- Protein: 6 g.
- Fiber: 4.9 g.

# 5. Cheesy Pesto Eggs with Tomatoes

**Preparation time:** 05 minutes

**Cooking time:** 05 minutes

**Servings:** 2

## Ingredients

- ½ cup basil pesto
- 2 eggs
- 2 oz. mozzarella
- 1 ripe tomato, sliced
- Red pepper flakes
- 2 pieces of toasted bread for serving

## Directions

1. In a nonstick pan, heat pesto on a low heat until it starts to bubble.
2. Add the eggs to the pan. Cover the pan and cook it on low heat for 2-3 minutes until the eggs white is set. Season it with salt, pepper, and red pepper flakes.
3. Take the pesto from the pan and spread it on the toast. Put tomatoes, cooked eggs, and cheese

## Nutrition

- Calories: 319
- Carbohydrates: 6.6 g
- Fats: 7.9 g
- Proteins: 14.3 g
- Fiber: 1.4 g

# 6. Spinach and Feta Frittata

**Preparation time:** 05 minutes
**Cooking time:** 15 minutes
**Servings:** 4

## Ingredients

- 4 eggs
- 1/8 cup milk
- ½ teaspoon dried oregano
- ¼ teaspoon black pepper
- ¼ teaspoon red chili flakes
- 1/8 teaspoon baking powder
- Pinch of kosher salt
- 6 oz. chopped spinach
- ¼ cup onion, finely chopped
- ½ chopped parsley
- 2 oz. crumbled feta cheese
- 1 tablespoon extra-virgin olive oil

## Directions

1. Preheat the oven to 375° F.
2. Take a mixing bowl and whisk eggs, baking powder, salt, pepper, oregano, and red chili flakes.
3. Add chopped parsley, spinach, and onions to the egg mixture.
4. Add olive oil in an oven-safe skillet and heat over medium flame for a few minutes. Pour the spinach and egg mixture and let it sit for 4-5 minutes on low flame. Transfer the pan to the oven.

## Nutrition

- Calories: 152
- Carbohydrates: 4.9 g.
- Fats: 10.7 g.

- Protein: 9.8 g
- Fiber: 1.4 g.

# 7. Eggs and Vegetable Casseroles

**Preparation time:** 15 minutes
**Cooking time:** 45 minutes
**Servings:** 3
**Ingredients**

- 2 eggs
- ¾ cup milk
- ¼ teaspoon red chili flakes
- 1/8 teaspoon oregano
- 1/8 teaspoon baking powder
- 1/8 teaspoon nutmeg powder
- Pinch of kosher salt and pepper
- 2 slices of bread, cut into ½ inch pieces
- 1 shallot thinly sliced
- 1 small tomato, sliced
- 1 oz. sliced mushrooms
- ½ oz. feta cheese
- ½ oz. olives
- 1 tablespoon olive oil
- ½ bell pepper, chopped

## Directions
1. Preheat the oven to 375° F. Adjust the middle rack in the oven.

44

2. Take a mixing bowl and whisk eggs, baking powder, salt, pepper, oregano, nutmeg, red chili flakes, and milk.
3. Add bread pieces, tomatoes, olives, cheese, and mushrooms to the egg mixture.
4. Brush olive oil in the casserole dish and pour the egg mixture. Place chopped bell peppers on the top.
5. Bake the mixture for 40-45 minutes.

## Nutrition

- Calories: 35
- Carbohydrates: 3.4 g.
- Fats: 2.3 g.
- Protein: 2 g
- Fiber: 0.4 g.

# 8. Greenly Apple Juice

**Preparation time:** 05 minutes
**Cooking time:** 0 minutes
**Servings:** 2

## Ingredients
- 1 bunch kale
- 1-inch piece fresh ginger, peeled
- 1 green apple
- 5 celery stalks, ends trimmed
- 1 large cucumber
- 1 oz. fresh parsley
- Handful leaves of mint
- 1 tablespoon lemon juice
- Pinch of salt and pepper
- 1 cup ice

## Directions
1. Blend all the ingredients in the blender until smooth.
2. Garnish with lemon wedges and mint leaves.

## Nutrition
- Calories: 92
- Carbohydrates: 21 g
- Fats: 0.8 g
- Protein: 2.8 g
- Fiber: 4 g

# Mediterranean Diet Lunch Recipes

# 9. Baked Balsamic Chicken

**Preparation time:** 10 minutes
**Cooking time:** 25 minutes
**Servings:** 3

## Ingredients

- $^{1/8}$ cup extra virgin olive oil
- 4 boneless and skinless chicken thighs
- ½ teaspoon table salt
- ½ tablespoon pepper
- 1 ½ tablespoon balsamic glaze
- ½ tablespoon tomato paste
- ½ teaspoon honey
- 1 ½ tablespoon lemon juice
- 2 garlic cloves
- ½ teaspoon thyme
- ½ teaspoon oregano
- ½ teaspoon sweet paprika

## Directions

1. Take a mixing bowl and whisk all the spices, balsamic glaze, and olive oil. Coat the chicken in the mixture.
2. Heat the oven to 425°F.
3. Transfer the chicken to the baking dish and bake it for 30 minutes.
4. Garnish the chicken with cilantro and lemon wedges.

## Nutrition

- Calories: 144
- Carbohydrates: 4 g
- Fats: 7.7 g
- Protein: 15 g
- Fiber: 1 g

# 10. Limey Cucumber Tomato Salad

**Preparation time:** 15 minutes
**Cooking time:** 0 minutes
**Servings:** 4
## Ingredients
- 2 cups Greek yogurt
- 1 cucumber, diced
- 2 tomatoes, diced
- 2 onions, diced
- ½ teaspoon black pepper
- 1 teaspoon kosher salt
- 1 tablespoon lime juice
- Handful leaves of mint and cilantro

## Directions
1. Take a large mixing bowl and combine all the ingredients until the vegetables are well coated with the yogurt.
2. Refrigerate for 10 minutes and enjoy.

## Nutrition
- Calories: 135
- Carbohydrates: 1.2 g
- Fats: 2.2 g
- Protein: 5.6 g
- Fiber: 1.8 g

# 11. Sardine and White Beans Salad

**Preparation time:** 15 minutes
**Cooking time:** 0 minutes
**Servings:** 2

## Ingredients
- ½ can of white beans, dried and rinsed
- 1 can sardines, chopped into squares
- ½ cup cherry tomatoes, cut in halves
- 1 green onion, finely chopped
- ½ jalapeno, deseeded and chopped
- ½ Italian fresh parsley
- 1 teaspoon mustard
- 1 tablespoon lime juice
- 1 garlic clove, minced
- 1 teaspoon, red pepper flakes
- ¼ cup of olive oil

## Directions
1. Combine olive oil, lemon juice, and spices in a bowl. Whisk it until smooth.
2. Take a large mixing bowl. Add sardines, chopped vegetables, and beans. Pour the spice mixture over it and toss it nicely to coat everything.

## Nutrition
- Calories: 120
- Carbohydrates: 10.45 g
- Fats: 4 g
- Protein: 11.35 g
- Fiber: 2.75 g

# 12. Limey Roasted Butternut Squash with Walnuts

**Preparation time:** 15 minutes

**Cooking time:** 05 minutes

**Servings:** 3

## Ingredients

- 1 ½ tablespoon olive oil
- 1 lb. butternut squash, peeled, halved, and seeded
- Pinch of fine sea salt and black pepper
- 1 ½ tablespoon fresh lime juice
- ¼ teaspoon finely grated lemon zest
- 2 garlic cloves. Minced
- ½ teaspoon crushed red pepper flakes
- ¼ chopped walnuts
- 1 green onion, thinly chopped

## Directions

1. Heat the oven at 425°F.
2. Oil a rimmed baking sheet and place the sliced butternut squash on it. Brush olive oil on it and sprinkle salt, chili flakes, and pepper.
3. Roast the squash for 20 minutes or until it turns golden brown on the top. Flip the sides and bake again for 8 to 10 minutes to make it tender.
4. Take a mixing bowl and prepare the vinaigrette. Add lime juice and zest, minced garlic, salt, and pepper. Mix it nicely and let it sit for 10 minutes.
5. Add olive oil to the vinaigrette and mix.
6. Pour the vinaigrette over the squash to coat all the slices.
7. Sprinkle scallions and walnuts.

### Nutrition

- Calories: 48
- Carbohydrates: 0.75 g
- Fats: 0.51 g
- Protein: 0.45 g
- Fiber: 0.3 g

# 13. Juicy, Herby, Garlicky Turkey Breast

**Preparation time:** 30 minutes

**Cooking time:** 45 minutes

**Servings:** 3

## Ingredients

- 1 lb. Bone-in turkey breast.
- 1 teaspoon fine sea salt
- ½ teaspoon ground allspice
- ½ teaspoon paprika
- ½ teaspoon pepper
- ¼ teaspoon nutmeg
- 7 garlic cloves, minced
- 1 oz. fresh parsley
- 4 shallots, peeled and halved
- 3 celery sticks, cut in halves
- 225 g/ ½ lb. grapes, red seedless
- ¾ cup extra-virgin olive oil
- Pinch of kosher salt or table salt

## Directions

1. Pat dry the turkey breast and season it with sea salt and pepper. Refrigerate it overnight to let the seasonings seep inside the flesh.
2. Preheat the oven to 425° F. Add grapes in a 9 x 13 baking pan. Drizzle 1 tablespoon olive oil and kosher/table salt. Roast the grapes for 10 minutes.
3. In a small bowl, mix all the spices and rub them over the turkey breast evenly.
4. Mix chopped parsley, garlic, and ½ cup olive oil in a bowl. Pour it over turkey breast. Spread it evenly on all the sides.
5. In the same baking pan, place shallots and celery to make the turkey bed. Place the turkey on the top. Roast the turkey for 45 minutes on 350° F.
6. After 40 minutes, remove the turkey and add in grapes. Let it roast for another 2 or 3 minutes more.
7. Slice the turkey and enjoy it with roasted vegetables and grapes.

## Nutrition

- Calories: 127

- Carbohydrates: 3.8 g
- Fats: 1.6 g
- Protein: 15.35 g
- Fiber: 0.52 g

# 14. Citrusy Rosemary Chicken

**Preparation time:** 10 minutes

**Cooking time:** 45 minutes

**Servings:** 3

## Ingredients

- 1 ½ lbs. chicken, cut into big pieces
- 1 teaspoon Kosher salt
- 1 cup white vinegar
- 1 orange zested and juiced, 1 orange sliced
- 2 tablespoon lemon juice, 1 lemon sliced
- 1 ½ tablespoon tomato paste
- ¾ teaspoon dried oregano
- ½ teaspoon rosemary
- ½ teaspoon sweet paprika
- 1 teaspoon black pepper
- ½ onion, sliced
- ½ tablespoon honey

## Directions

1. Season the chicken with salt and pepper and refrigerate for 1 hour.
2. Prepare the citrus marinade by mixing vinegar, orange and lemon zest, lime juice and zest, olive oil, tomato paste, spices, garlic, and onion. Whisk well to combine.
3. Coat the chicken in this marinade and refrigerate it for at least 30 minutes.
4. Preheat the oven to 425° F.
5. Transfer the chicken to the braising pan with the marinade. Roast the chicken for 30 minutes.
6. In a small bowl, mix together olive oil and honey. Brush it on the roasted chicken.

7. Switch the oven to broil function. Broil the chicken for 4-5 minutes to get a crisp golden layer on the top.
8. Place the chicken on a platter and garnish it with lime and orange slices. Sprinkle salt and lemon juice to give it a tangy flavor.

## Nutrition

- Calories: 159.35
- Carbohydrates: 5.8 g
- Fats: 2.85 g
- Protein: 12.4 g
- Fiber: 1.45 g

# Mediterranean Diet
# Dinner Recipes

# 15. Baked Cranberry Chicken Recipe

**Preparation time:** 15 minutes
**Cooking time:** 45 minutes
**Servings:** 3

## Ingredients

- 1 cup fresh cranberries
- ¼ cup brown sugar
- 3 tablespoon white vinegar
- 4 chicken breast
- 4 garlic cloves
- Pinch of salt and pepper
- 1 teaspoon dry rosemary
- ½ teaspoon paprika
- ¼ extra virgin olive oil
- 2 tablespoon lemon juice
- 1 medium-sized onion, sliced
- 2 celery stalks, chopped
- ½ chicken broth
- Lemon wedges for garnish

## Directions

1. Pat dry chicken pieces and season them with salt.
2. In a mixing bowl, combine oil, vinegar, brown sugar, lemon juice, and spices. With clean hands, apply the mixture over chicken pieces. Make sure to coat it evenly.
3. Preheat the oven to 425° F. Transfer the chicken, marinade, celery, and onion into an oiled baking pan.
4. Add ½ cup chicken broth and cranberries to the baking pan and bake for 40 minutes.
5. Serve hot with plain brown rice and lemon wedges.

## Nutrition

- Calories: 145.2
- Carbohydrates: 4.5 g
- Fats: 6.2 g
- Protein: 0.7 g
- Fiber: 1.3 g

# 16. Mediterranean Salmon Burgers

**Preparation time:** 15 minutes
**Cooking time:** 5 minutes
**Servings:** 2
## Ingredients
- 1 lb. Salmon fillet, cut into chunks
- 1 teaspoon Dijon mustard
- 1.5 tablespoon onion paste
- ½ cup chopped parsley
- 1 teaspoon ground coriander
- ¼ teaspoon sweet paprika
- ½ teaspoon black pepper
- ½ teaspoon Kosher salt
- ¼ extra virgin olive oil
- ¼ cup breadcrumbs for coating
- 1 lemon
- 2 tablespoon chili sauce
- 3 oz. baby arugula
- 1 red onion, finely sliced
- 3 whole-wheat buns

## Directions
1. Add about ¼ of the salmon and mustard to the processor. Run the processor to make the salmon pasty.
2. Take the remaining salmon and process it until it's coarsely chopped.
3. Combine salmon, onion paste, parsley, lemon juice, and all the spices. Mix well and refrigerate for 1 hour.
4. After 1 hour, grease your hand and make 1-inch salmon burger patties from the mixture.
5. Coat them with breadcrumbs and proceed towards frying.
6. Heat the olive oil. Fry the salmon patties from both sides for 4-5 minutes on medium-low flame.
7. Layout the patties on a paper towel to drain the excess oil.
8. Spread the chili sauce on the bun. Place the fried salmon patty, baby arugula, onions, and tomato slices.

## Nutrition

- Calories: 68.5
- Carbohydrates: 2.1 g
- Fats: 7 g
- Protein: 1 g
- Fiber: 1.7 g

# 17. Grilled Eggplant with Feta Cheese

**Preparation time:** 30 minutes

**Cooking time:** 10 minutes

**Servings:** 3

## Ingredients

- 1 globe eggplant, cut into ½ inches round slices
- Pinch of fine sea salt or table salt
- ½ cup extra virgin olive oil
- 1 garlic, minced
- 1 tablespoon lime juice
- ½ jalapeno, deseeded and chopped
- Whipped Feta Cheese

## Directions

1. Lay down the eggplant slices on a large tray lined with a paper towel. Generously sprinkle salt and let it sit for 30 minutes.
2. In a mixing bowl, add lime juice, ¼ cup olive oil, garlic, and jalapeno. Add a pinch of salt and let it sit for 10 minutes.
3. Wipe the water droplets and excessive salt from the eggplant slices.
4. Heat the gas grill and brush oil on its grates. Let the grates heat up before placing the eggplant slices.
5. Brush the eggplant slices with olive oil. Place the oiled side on the grates and let it grill for 4 to 5 minutes or until the charred marks appear on the eggplant slices.
6. Brush the other side with olive oil and place it down on the grates.
7. Place the eggplant slices on a platter and pour over the olive oil, garlic, and jalapeno mixture.

8. Serve the grilled slices with warm pita bread pieces and whipped feta.

## Nutrition

- Calories: 53
- Carbohydrates: 3.3 g
- Fats: 7.15 g
- Protein: 0.5 g
- Fiber: 1.45 g

# 18. Tahini Cauliflower Wraps

**Preparation time:** 10 minutes

**Cooking time:** 35 minutes

**Servings:** 2

## Ingredients

- ½ cup tahini paste
- 1 large cauliflower, cut into small florets
- 2 tablespoon olive oil
- 1 teaspoon kosher salt
- 2 teaspoon red chili flakes
- 1 teaspoon paprika
- ½ teaspoon cumin powder
- 2 tablespoon lemon juice
- 1 red onion, thinly sliced
- 1 cup chickpeas, boiled
- Lettuce wraps

## Directions

1. Pat dry the cauliflower florets with a paper towel.
2. Combine all the spices, 1 tablespoon olive oil, 1 tablespoon lemon juice, and all the spices. Coat the florets in this mixture.
3. Roast the florets for 20 minutes at 425° F. flip and turn the sides of the florets and another roast for 10 minutes.

4. Squeeze remaining lemon juice on roasted florets.
5. Take the lettuce wrap and spread the tahini paste over it. Top it with onions, chickpeas, and cauliflower florets. Wrap it and serve with Greek yogurt or chili garlic sauce.

## Nutrition
- Calories: 245
- Carbohydrates: 48.5 g
- Fats: 3.3g
- Protein: 11.6 g
- Fiber: 11.4 g

# 19. Baked Italian Meatballs with Veggies

**Preparation time:** 20 minutes
**Cooking time:** 20 minutes
**Servings:** 4

## Ingredients
- 1 red onion, thinly sliced in rounds
- ½ lb. baby potatoes
- 6 bell peppers, julienne cut
- 5 garlic cloves, minced
- 3 teaspoon dried oregano
- 2 teaspoon Kosher salt and white pepper
- ½ cup extra virgin olive oil
- 1 lb. cherry tomatoes
- 1 lb. lean ground turkey
- 1 yellow onion, finely chopped
- 1 cup fresh parsley, finely chopped
- ¼ grated Parmesan cheese

- ¼ Italian breadcrumbs
- 1 egg

## Directions

1. Preheat the oven to 400° F.
2. Combine all the vegetables (*except yellow onion*), 2 minced garlic, 1 teaspoon oregano, ½ teaspoon salt, and pepper. Add 1 tablespoon olive oil and toss all the vegetables. Place the vegetables on the greased pan.
3. Take another mixing bowl and combine the remaining ingredient. Grease your hands and make 1-inch meatballs.
4. Place the meatballs on the same pan as vegetables. Drizzle the remaining olive oil.
5. Cover the sheet pan with aluminum foil. Bake the meatballs and veggies for 15 minutes.
6. Remove the foil and bake again for 5 minutes.
7. Serve with cauliflower rice and cucumber slices.

## Nutrition

- Calories: 340
- Carbohydrates: 27.6 g
- Fats: 20.8 g
- Proteins: 27.5 g
- Fiber: 5.3 g

# 20. Herby Moroccan Sandwiches

**Preparation time:** 5 minutes
**Cooking time:** 0 minutes
**Servings:** 4

## Ingredients

- 1 cup fresh parsley
- 1 cup fresh cilantro
- 1 clove garlic
- ½ teaspoon ground coriander
- 1 ½ teaspoon red chili flakes
- ½ teaspoon dried ginger
- ½ teaspoon kosher salt
- 1 tablespoon lemon juice
- ½ cup extra virgin olive oil
- Multigrain bread slices
- 1 large onion, sliced
- 1 tomato, sliced
- Parmesan cheese, as per your liking

## Directions

1. Blend all the herbs, spices, and olive oil in a food processor until smooth.
2. Spread the herby mixture on the bread slice.
3. Top it with onion, tomatoes, and sprinkle grated cheese. Top it with another bread slice and enjoy.

## Nutrition

- Calories: 120
- Carbohydrates: 5 g
- Fats: 19.2 g
- Protein: 0.6 g
- Fiber: 0.4 g

# Anti-Inflammatory Diet

## Reduce Inflammation by Making
## The Right Dietary Changes

# Chapter 1. Introduction to Anti-Inflammatory Diet

The anti-inflammatory diet is the most buzzed-about and hyped-up diet in the world of nutrition. It is helpful for people suffering from inflammation.

Before we discuss this diet more, the food groups it suggests eating, its benefits, etc., it is important to fully understand the term *'Inflammation.'*

When we come across the term inflammation, our mind flashes the images of swelled and red skin. Inflammation is more than just skin getting red and hot. Swelling and redness are the external signs of inflammation. There are many other internal signs of inflammation. Moreover, inflammation gives rise to many other diseases and disrupts the person's overall health.

## What is Inflammation?

Inflammation is our immune system's response to fight an infection or injury. When infection-causing bacteria or viruses enter the body, the inflammatory cells become active and come to the rescue.

The inflammatory cells try to protect the immune system and enable the body to curb the damage from infection. This often results in swelling, redness, and sometimes even slight pain. These signs are perfectly normal, as long as it subsides after some time.

However, if the inflammation never fully goes away, it is not a good sign. This state is known as chronic inflammation. This means the body is at high alert to fight off bacteria, infections, injuries, etc., even when there are no potential risks or threats to the system. Chronic inflammation contributes to some major health issues such as heart diseases, diabetes, Alzheimer's. In severe cases, it can also trigger various types of cancers.

Fortuitously, inflammation is not entirely uncontrollable. A person can control the inflammation level to some extent. For instance, certain habits and lifestyles trigger high inflammation levels. Suppose a person makes positive changes to his lifestyle, such as giving up smoking and drinking alcohol. In that case, he can see a change in his inflammation levels. Furthermore, if he changes his diet, the redness, swelling, and pain will eventually subside. The body will return to the normal inflammation level.

Doctors also suggest some medication to manage the severe pain that results from inflammation. However, pain killers and medication drugs aren't free of side effects. The majority of these drugs cause fogginess, weariness, and prolonged use can also cause memory loss.

Thanks to the anti-inflammatory diet, managing and recovering from high inflammation level is possible.

# What is Anti-Inflammatory Diet?

As the name suggests, *Anti-Inflammatory* this diet lowers and prevents high inflammation levels.

The anti-inflammatory diet is rich in fruits, vegetables, omega-3 fatty acids, lean proteins, whole grains, and natural ground spices. Just like the Mediterranean diet, this diet also limits and discourages red meat, alcohol, sugary foods and beverages, and alcohol.

The reason behind the limitation of certain food groups in this diet is that they can worsen the inflammation. Moreover, they can work as a catalyst to speed up the development of certain diseases.

An anti-inflammatory diet includes whole, natural, and unprocessed foods. Fruits and vegetables are rich in vitamins, minerals, and antioxidants.

Antioxidants are immensely helpful to cure inflammation. They remove the free radicals in the body. Free radicals are formed naturally as byproducts of the body's metabolism. These radicals are also formed due to some external factors, which include:

- Using the cooking oil that has been heated several times
- Stress
- Smoking
- Diet loaded with junk and processed food

Free radicals damage cells, which in return heightens the inflammation level and triggers many diseases.

By adopting the anti-inflammatory diet, the high levels of inflammation drop back to the normal range and prevent its diseases.

# Chapter 2. Benefits of Anti-Inflammatory Diet

The anti-inflammatory diet is helpful for normalizing the high inflammation levels and provides plenty of other benefits. The reason behind it is the food groups that this diet includes, especially foods rich in antioxidants.

Let's have a look at the wonders that an anti-inflammatory diet can do for your immune system and overall well-being.

## What can Anti-inflammatory Diet do to the Body?

### 1. Treats Inflammation

The first benefit of an anti-inflammatory diet is that it treats inflammation. The high antioxidant diet clears the free radicals from our immune system. Our body often mistakes it as an infection or harmful substance.

Adopting an anti-inflammatory diet will reduce the external sign of inflammation, such as redness, swelling, irritation, and itching on the skin surface.

This diet limits processed and sugary foods; this helps the person get rid of unwanted heaps of fat. The calorie deficit resulting from this diet helps in weight loss.

### 2. Helps in Shedding Weight

An anti-inflammatory diet promotes foods that are natural and unprocessed. Processed and sugary foods increase the glucose level. The body uses the energy and stores the remaining glucose as fat reserves. Increased intake of processed foods and inactive lifestyle contributes to unhealthy weight gain.

Making dietary changes and eating antioxidant-rich fruits and veggies, combined with fatty omega acid, promotes fat loss. The intake of protein also keeps our muscles healthy and energetic. The increased muscle mass means more calories are burnt when the muscles are moved. Burning more calories than consuming them directly affects weight.

### 3. Promotes Heart Health

An anti-inflammatory diet includes foods with omega fatty acids. These acids are healthy for the heart. Eating omega fatty acids can help your heart in the following ways:

- Omega fatty acids reduce the triglyceride in the blood. This improves the cholesterol level and prevents bad cholesterol from building up in the body.
- It improves the heartbeat and treats the problem of rapid or irregular heartbeat.
- It controls the buildup of plaque in the arteries so that they aren't hardened.
- Fatty acids also prevent blockage in the arteries.

## 4. Reduces the Risk of Diabetes

Sugary foods and carbs are the primary culprits for diabetes disease. Adopting a healthy anti-inflammatory diet reduces the consumption of carbs and sugar. Moreover, this diet promotes the intake of healthy snacks, such as nuts, seeds, and natural spices.

The reduction of sugar and carbs in the diet improves the blood sugar level and normalizes insulin levels. This diet is helpful for prediabetes patients. Adopting this diet can reverse the problem of diabetes.

## 5. Improves Skin and Hair Texture

Poor diet, lack of physical activity, and poor quality sleep harm the body from inside and from outside.

When free radicals and other toxins increase in our body, it affects our skin and causes a number of problems. Poor diet and sedentary lifestyle are also linked with baldness and hair fall problems.

A person can easily reverse the problems of skin and hair by making a healthy dietary change. Intake of vitamins, minerals, and antioxidants can do wonders for the skin. It can slow down the signs of aging. Consuming fruits and vegetables are proven to restore the glow and elasticity in the skin, which often depletes with age.

## 6. Lowers Cholesterol

Processed food contains a high level of sugar, salts, and other preservatives. All these things promote the buildup of LDL, which is bad cholesterol in our body. The increased cholesterol sticks to the arteries' walls and makes it difficult for the blood to pass through them.

Limiting the intake of processed foods and switching to natural alternatives increases HDL, which is good cholesterol. It lowers down LDL to allow the blood to pass easily through the arteries.

This, in return, also helps to lower the high blood pressure.

## 7. Lowers Down High Blood Pressure

When bad cholesterol lines up on the side of the arteries, it obstructs the flow of blood circulation. The heart has to exert extra pressure than normal to pass the blood in the arteries. The arteries provide a narrow passage for the blood to pass. The heart has to work harder to supply the blood. This gives rise to the blood pressure from the normal range.
Making simple changes in the diet can help remove the bad cholesterol in the arteries and clear up blood. The heart will not have to exert extra pressure to circulate the blood. This will help lower down the pressure on the heart, and blood will pass easily through the arteries.

## 8. Improves Metabolism

Slow metabolism contributes to obesity. It also slows down the other bodily functions and recovery from a disease or an injury.
An anti-inflammatory diet includes all the nutrients and minerals that promote heart health and boost metabolism.
Increased metabolism enables the body to use more energy and speeds up the healing from a disease, infection, or injury.

## 9. Prevents Cancer

The unique characteristic that differentiates this diet from other diets is the intake of antioxidants.
Antioxidants clear our body from free radicals that are harmful to health and trigger many severe diseases, including cancer.
When the body is free from radicals, the chances of developing cancer become minimal.

## 10.   Promotes Active Lifestyle

A healthy diet promotes an active lifestyle. It enables the person to enjoy life with full energy and without any chronic disease.
The anti-inflammatory diet is remarkable for losing weight and keeping the body fit. A person can lead an active lifestyle and enjoy good physical and cognitive health.

# Chapter 3. Anti-Inflammatory Diet and Menopause

The previous 2 sections have covered in detail the following parts:

What is menopause?

Symptoms of Menopause?

Effect of Menopause on Women's life

And, why do women gain weight during menopause?

It wouldn't be wrong to say Menopause is the toughest part of a women's life. Her body undergoes a substantial change, both externally and physically. She gains weight, battles with anxiety, and deals with many other body problems.

However, there's one more thing that comes with menopause: Increased Inflammation. Due to the drop in hormone levels, the inflammation level in the body rises and triggers the development of discomfort and many other diseases.

Many females over 50 are prescribed hormone therapy to prevent inflammation or to normalize its level. But there is another safer and effective method to combat the high inflammation levels that result from menopause. It is to make simple lifestyle and dietary changes to solve the inflammation issue.

## Understanding the Link between High Inflammation and Menopause

Estrogen is a hormone that also acts as an anti-inflammatory. When females menstruate, their estrogen works as an anti-inflammatory and prevents the surge in inflammation level.

As the body enters the menopause or even premenopausal state, the estrogen level depletes. Its capacity to work as an anti-inflammatory reduces, and as a result, the inflammation level increases. With that, the risk of cardiovascular diseases, diabetes, and deterioration of mental health also increase manifold.

Apart from inflammation, depleting hormones also trigger many other health issues. Let's have a look at them:

## Risk of Health Issues in Menopause

The reason why women become the victim of health issues in their menopausal phase is because of the low levels of hormones. Before menopause, hormone levels are normal. They work together to protect the body from numerous diseases and health issues.

Hormones like:
- DHEA
- Estrogen
- Pregnenolone
- Progesterone

Significantly drop as the body ages. The low levels become incapable of protecting the body as they used to previously.

Let's shine a light on the health issues triggered by the drop in hormones:

# 1. Bone Health

Women in the premenopausal, menopausal, and postmenopausal stages are at increased risk of weaker bones.

This is because a group of cells called Osteoclasts helps in healing and growing bones. It breaks down the bone tissues and releases its mineral into the blood. It is an important process as it maintains the calcium level in the blood.

However, tables turn when the process of resorption, i.e., the breaking of bone tissues, increases. This makes the bone weaker and prone to damage. When the inflammation levels are higher, the T cells in the body will recruit and extend the life of the Osteoclasts through IL-6 (*Interleukin-6*). The estrogen in the body controls the inhibition of IL-6. When the body has lesser estrogen, it is incapable of inhibiting IL-6 and prolonging the life of Osteoclasts. As a result, the process of resorption (*Breaking of bone tissues*) increases, and bones become fragile. The women suffer from Osteoporosis and can easily damage their bones from even the smallest injury.

# 2. Joint Health

The weakening of bones due to the increased dissolution of bone tissues also affects the joints. This increases the development of arthritis and osteoarthritis.

A drop in estrogen levels raises inflammation and affects the integrity of joints in the body.

# 3. Muscle Health

Estrogen, the important hormone, also affects our muscle mass and its strength. In menopause, the muscle mass rapidly declines. Furthermore, it affects muscles strength to carry out strenuous physical tasks.

This is perhaps the reason why females feel lethargic and drained after any rigorous physical activity. Moreover, muscular pain, body aches, loss of bone density is pretty common in women over 50.

## 4. Brain Health

Another area of health that is affected after menopause is brain health. In chronic neuroinflammation, the body keeps the microglia cells activated so that they produce inflammatory cytokines and clear damaged neurons.
If the microglia cells are continuously active, it disturbs the brain's health. It incites the development of multiple cognitive diseases such as:

- Alzheimer
- Parkinson
- Multiple sclerosis

The estrogen hormone controls the activation of microglia cells. In the absence of proper estrogen hormone, the cells remain activated and expose the brain to degenerative diseases. Estrogen also protects our brain from brain fog, which is also caused by microglial cells.
Another hormone, which affects our brain is Pregnenolone. It is a steroid hormone produced by the brain and is referred to as a neurosteroid.
Neurosteroid is responsible for regulating mood and memory. It also serves as neuroplastic, neuroprotective, and neurogenesis roles. Lower pregnenolone level is often related to depression, memory issues, and fluctuation in hormone levels.
DHEA, another essential hormone, directly affects brain health. A decrease in DHEA is associated with Alzheimer's and Dementia.
Many females battle with anxiety and depression during perimenopause and menopause due to the drop in hormone levels directly connected with our brain health.
Another health issue associated with low hormone levels in females is...

## 5. Weight Gain

The most common health issue after menopause is unhealthy weight gain in females. Women's body stores fat in their buttocks and thighs. But after menopause, the body starts piling up fat in the abdominal area, called '*visceral fat.*' This fat is highly inflammatory. Abdominal obesity triggers multiple diseases such as high levels of bad cholesterol, increased blood pressure, and diabetes.
All these health issues can be resolved to certain levels by making lifestyle and dietary changes. An anti-inflammatory diet can be full of help for females struggling in their menopause phase. The diet is rich in antioxidants. It will normalize the high inflammation levels. Moreover, it will preserve the cognitive, muscle, and bone health of females.

# Importance of Anti-Inflammatory Diet for Menopause

The following nutrients and minerals included in the anti-inflammatory diet are super helpful for women dealing with the symptoms of Menopause.

## 1. Vitamin-D

You might be surprised to read this: 'Vit-D is not only a fat-soluble vitamin but also a hormone.'

An anti-inflammatory diet promotes eating cod liver oil, fatty fish, and eggs. It also allows small portions of red meat in the diet. All these food items are a good source of vitamin D. Our body also absorbs sunlight, which is then turned into Vitamin D with some process. As the body ages, its ability to convert sunlight into vitamin D decreases.

It is highly recommended to get your vitamin D levels checked if you are above 50 or entered the phase of menopause. With an anti-inflammatory diet, you can fill up your body with the required vitamin D. If a person's vitamin D levels are low, the doctor might prescribe them Vitamin D supplements.

The deficiency of Vitamin D increases inflammation, causes bone weakening and other heart issues.

## 2. Boron

Seeing the element Boron on this list might have reminded you of your chemistry books in high school. Boron is not only found in the periodic table. It is also present in the food we eat.

An anti-inflammatory diet includes food that is rich in boron. Foods such as leafy vegetables, raisins, nuts, prunes, coffee, beans, potatoes, and non-citrus fruits contain boron.

Boron is an important element for human health. It prevents calcium loss and bone demineralization. It extends the life of Vitamin D and estrogen in our body so that they last longer in our body and continue to provide their benefits to the body. Several studies have shown that Boron also plays a vital role in brain health.

## 3. Omega-3 Fatty Acids

Omega 3-fatty acids are polyunsaturated fatty acids. The body is unable to make these fatty acids on its own. Thus, it must be supplied to the body through our diet.

Omega 3-fatty acids have 3 main types:
- Alpha-linoleic Acid (*ALA*)
- Docosahexaenoic acid (*DHA*)
- Eicosapentaenoic acid (*EPA*)

Alpha-linoleic acid is present in flax seeds, flaxseed oil, chia seeds, hemp seeds, and walnuts. Docosahexaenoic acid is found in fish oil, fatty fish, meat, eggs, and dairy products. Eicosapentaenoic acid is present in animal products, such as meat, milk, and fish oil. Omega 3 fatty acids are extremely helpful for maintaining cognitive health and inflammation levels. The presence of omega 3-fatty acids reduces the inflammatory factors in the body.

## 4. Curcumin

Another element that is found in an anti-inflammatory diet is Curcumin. It is a powerful anti-inflammatory substance. It is also rich in antioxidants. Turmeric, a famous Asian spice, is loaded with Curcumin.

In Asian cuisines, turmeric is used to give curries and rice a natural yellow tint. Moreover, many Asian households mix a teaspoon of turmeric in warm milk or water to heal the injuries and treat the cold.

Curcumin's antioxidant and anti-inflammatory effects prevent cancer, cough, and cold. Curcumin also treats the neuro conditions, such as Dementia, Alzheimer's, and depression. In menopause, the risk of diabetes is quite evident for women. Consuming Curcumin can prevent the development of diabetes.

## 5. Resveratrol

Resveratrol belongs to a group of plant compounds which are known as polyphenols. This compound group acts as an antioxidant. Resveratrol is found in seeds and skins of red grapes and berries. Japanese knotweed is known as the powerhouse of resveratrol.

This element has dual properties; it works as an antioxidant as well as an anti-inflammatory. Many women complain about body pain, mood swings, and other mental health issues in the postmenopausal phase. The inclusion of resveratrol in an anti-inflammatory diet can prove to be helpful for soothing pain and improving mood.

## 6. *Glutathione*

Finally, it's time to talk about the mother of all the antioxidants, i.e., *Glutathione*. Glutathione is also known as *Master Antioxidant.* It is present in human cells and tissues. Glutathione is required to activate other antioxidants like Vitamin C and Vitamin E in the body. Glutathione's primary function is to protect the cells and tissues from oxidation damage. In the absence of this important antioxidant, the cells in the body will function poorly, get damaged, and eventually die. This will result in the development of many acute and degenerative diseases.

# Top Anti-Inflammatory Foods for Dealing with Menopause

## 1. Fruits and Vegetables

An anti-inflammatory diet encourages a hefty portion of fruits and veggies in the daily meal plan.

Fruits and veggies are full of vitamins and minerals and provide essential antioxidants and fiber to keep the body moving.

The top fruits and vegetables with a high level of antioxidants include:

- Leafy green vegetables
- Tomatoes
- Beets
- Berries
- Broccoli
- Avocados
- Oranges
- Tangerines
- Lemon
- Apple


## 2. Whole-Grains

Whole grains are a good source of fiber. The proper intake of fiber improves the bowel system and lowers C-reactive protein in the blood. Swap the high carbs grains with the following ones:
- Oatmeal
- Wild rice
- Brown rice
- Millet
- Quinoa

## 3.  Omega-3 Fatty Acids

An anti-inflammatory diet is rich in Omega 3-Fatty acids. These acids are the best friend of the heart. It reduces inflammation, lowers cholesterol, and improves the blood insulin level. Fish is an excellent source of omega-3 fatty acids. It prevents inflammation and slows down the production of pro-inflammatory compounds in the body.
Include the following fish in your lunches and dinner:
* Anchovies
* Herring
* Mackerel
* Salmon
* Sardines

## 4. Legumes

Legumes are the powerhouse of fiber and magnesium. Both these nutrients are excellent for reducing inflammation. Introduce the following items in your diet and watch it reduce your inflammation:
* Black, red, and pinto beans
* Chickpeas
* Lentil
* Soy: Tofu and edamame

## 5. Dark Chocolate

Being on a diet doesn't mean you cannot tantalize your taste buds with chocolate, right?
The anti-inflammatory diet encourages dieters to eat a piece of dark chocolate. Unlike milk chocolates, dark chocolate has high cocoa content. It contains flavanol contain fights pro-inflammatory compounds, and prevents inflammation in the body.
Before buying the dark chocolate, make sure to get the one that has 70% or more cocoa content.

## 6. Nuts and Seeds

Just as the Mediterranean diet encourages the consumption of nuts and seeds, an anti-inflammatory diet recommends the same.

Eating nuts and seeds in a salad or as snacks fuels up the body with numerous antioxidants. It curbs appetite and also increases the good cholesterol in the body.

Keep the stock of the following nuts and seeds for hunger pangs at odd hours:

- Almonds
- Cashew
- Chestnut
- Walnuts
- Pistachios
- Roasted grams
- Pine nuts
- Hazelnuts
- Pumpkin seeds
- Sunflower seeds
- Sesame seeds

## 7. Green Tea

Green tea contains 0 calories. This makes it an ideal choice for dieters than the regular tea and creamed coffees. Caffeine is also a culprit to increase inflammation. Switching to green tea will keep all the calories away and lower down the caffeine in the blood.

Green tea is rich in antioxidants and flavonoids. It flushes toxins from the body, improves metabolism and digestion.

## 8. Spices and Oil

Ginger and turmeric are spices rich in anti-inflammatory properties. Include a good amount of ginger and turmeric in your dishes to get a good dose of antioxidants.

Regular cooking oils do not provide anti-inflammatory properties. Hence, switch to using avocado oil or extra virgin olive oil for cooking your meals. Both the oils contain a high level of antioxidants that are beneficial for controlling the high inflammation level in the body.

# Chapter 4. Keto Anti-Inflammatory Diet

The famous keto diet used by plenty of celebrities and health experts is beneficial for weight loss and equally helpful for reducing inflammation.

The Keto diet is high in good fats and low on carbs. This puts the body in a ketosis state, where our body switches from carbs for energy to fats. The fat stored in our body is used as energy, and as a result, the body loses weight.

Sugar is inflammatory. The spike in blood sugar level can worsen the inflammation, leading to more swelling, redness, irritation, and severe pain. Increased intake of sugar and carbs produces free radicals that inflame the blood vessel's linings and trigger the body's immunity to respond. This leads to increased inflammation.

A Keto Anti-inflammatory diet puts the body in ketosis. Both Keto and anti-inflammatory diets restrict carbs and include good fats, protein, and other vitamin-rich foods.

By onboarding the keto diet and including the foods recommended in an anti-inflammatory diet, you will get the best of both worlds. You will lose weight and lower down the inflammation in your blood vessels and reduce the pain that results from it.

Include good fats such as olive oil, avocado oil, peanut butter, etc., in your diet to shift your body to burning fats in the body instead of carbs from the food.

# Chapter 5. Anti-Inflammatory Mediterranean Diet

In the previous section, we discussed The Mediterranean diet in detail. We covered everything from its origin, basis, benefits, and the food groups included.

The Mediterranean diet is not different from the Anti-inflammatory diet. In fact, the food groups included in the Mediterranean diet are rich in antioxidants and fight inflammation. Comparing the food items of both diets, researchers have concluded that the Mediterranean diet and anti-inflammatory diet are more or less similar. The only exception is that the Mediterranean diet allows the consumption of wine in meal plans. Whereas the anti-inflammatory diet restricts the use of alcohol in meals.

Both diets encourage the consumption of plenty of fruits, veggies, whole grains, fish, herbs, spices, nuts, and seeds. These food items are not only rich in nutrients and minerals. Still, they are also packed with necessary antioxidants to fight inflammation.

If a person is suffering from the problem of inflammation, he can onboard the Mediterranean diet too. Because the results of both diets are similar. The only change that the person will have to make is to give up drinking wine, which worsens the inflammation.

The common food items in both the diets are listed as follows:

- Cherries
- Spinach
- Avocado
- Ginger
- Chia seeds
- Berries: Strawberries, Goji berries, blackberries
- Orange
- Lemons
- Turmeric
- Thyme
- Oregano
- Garlic
- Avocado oil
- Olives
- Extra virgin Olive Oil
- Mint
- Anchovies
- Salmon
- Mackerel
- Sardines
- Kale
- Spinach
- Lettuce

If you are on the Mediterranean diet, then cut away alcohol and Viola! You are following an Anti-inflammatory diet.

# Chapter 6. Anti-Inflammatory Diet with Intermittent Fasting

Remember the detailed section on intermittent fasting and its benefits?

Intermittent fasting is a useful tool to put the body to ketosis, i.e., to burn stored fat for energy instead of sugar from the food.

During ketosis, our body gets rid of toxic and irreparable cells. Moreover, it is clear that free radicals in our bodies contribute to the development of cancers and many other diseases. During ketosis, our body also lowers down the inflammation level.

Combining an anti-inflammatory diet with intermittent fasting will help the body to heal the inflammation faster. It will bring back the inflammation levels to normal.

After your fasting period is over, break your fast by consuming antioxidant-rich foods. It will instantly charge up your body, satiate your hunger, normalize your blood pressure, prevent diabetes, and keep the risk of cancers and tumors at bay.

Let's discuss the benefits of an Anti-Inflammatory diet combined with Intermittent Fasting:

## 1. Reduces Inflammation

There are plenty of studies that support the fact that intermittent fasting reduces inflammation. When the body goes without food for a good number of hours, it goes into a ketosis state. During this state, the body relies on the stored fats for energy. It uses and burns the fat reserves and generates energy to carry out bodily functions.

While the body is in a Ketosis state, it also clears away its free radicals and unwanted toxins. This, in return, lowers the inflammation levels as the body doesn't have to treat the free radicals as a threat to immunity.

## 2. Helps in Weight Loss

Intermittent Fasting is an excellent tool to make the body use stored fat for energy. However, stuffing up yourself with junk and fried food will bring back all the calories to the body. Intermittent fasting will help lose weight only when the body doesn't get extra calories than what it burns. Including an anti-inflammatory diet will prevent the dieter from filling himself up with junk and calorie-dense food. The intake of antioxidants and mineral-dense food will fuel up the cells and tissue and speed up the weight loss process. Moreover, an anti-inflammatory diet includes a wide variety of food groups. You can enjoy all the food groups without depriving yourself of anything.

81

## 3. Prevents the Development of Cancers

As discussed in the previous paragraphs that intermittent fasting clears the free radicals from the body. These free radicals are often associated with the development of several cancers in the body.

Fasting clears the radicals, and the anti-inflammatory diet energizes the cells with antioxidants. The antioxidants protect cells, tissues, and organs. Moreover, it prevents the development of cancers in the body.

Combining the best of both the fasting and the anti-inflammatory diet, the threat of cancer will stay at bay, and a person can live an active and healthy life.

## 4. Restores Glow and Elasticity to Skin

The anti-inflammatory diet is rich in fruits, vegetables, grains, legumes, nuts, and seeds. These food items supply loads of vitamins, nutrients, minerals, and antioxidants to the body.

These nutrients are super helpful for skin, hair, and nails. The intake of fruits, veggies, and protein daily restores the glow back to the skin.

When women enter the menopause stage, the aging process speeds up. Their glow fades away, nails become brittle, and the hair loses its shine and volume. Embarking the anti-inflammatory diet can help the women in their menopause to rewind the aging process and appear and feel more youthful.

## 5. Improves Overall Health

An anti-inflammatory diet provides ample minerals, vitamins, calcium, protein, and antioxidants to the body.

All these things are essential for a healthy body. The anti-inflammatory diet is helpful for bones health, muscle health, brain health, and even improve mood.

Making an Anti-inflammatory diet a part of your life will keep you active, free from diseases, and fit. So that you can live your life to the fullest without worrying about the diseases.

# Chapter 7. Sample Meal Plan for Anti-Inflammatory Diet

If you are planning to onboard this excellent diet, the following meal plan can help you get started.

The meal includes all the food groups so that you take a balanced and filling diet every day. This meal plan is presented as a sample. You can tweak changes in it and adjust the meals according to your taste, likes, and preferences.

| Day | Breakfast | Lunch | Dinner |
| --- | --- | --- | --- |
| 1 | 1 cup black tea and Strawberry banana oats | Green salad with sliced carrots and Tahini dip, a small bowl of blackberries | Walnut Rosemary Crusted Salmon with roasted squash |
| 2 | Raspberry Yogurt Smoothie | Baked or Air fried chicken strips seasoned with salt, pepper, and paprika | Tuna Sandwich with roasted cauliflower |
| 3 | Walnut and blueberry yogurt parfait with 1 cup of green tea | Zucchini Noodles with turkey meatballs and spinach | Stir-fried brown rice with sautéed carrots, capsicum, onion, cauliflower, cabbage, and chicken |
| 4 | Chocolate and Chia Pudding | Cauliflower rice with baked salmon | Stir-fried red beans with vinegar and green chilies, and brown rice |
| 5 | 1 tall glass of turmeric latte | Boiled eggs and avocado sandwich | Garlic shrimps with broccoli, spinach, and quinoa |
| 6 | Scrambled eggs and a handful of almonds | Boiled chickpeas with a hearty topping of chopped onion, tomato, spring onion, green chilies, and a dash of lime. | Grilled chicken breast with vegetable salsa |

| 7 | 1 cup green tea with apple slices and a handful of nuts | Chicken and lettuce wraps | Fish steak with whole wheat pasta |

# Chapter 8. Tips To Lose Weight and Gain Vitality with Anti-Inflammatory Diet

The following tips will help you onboard an anti-inflammatory diet and shed the excess fat off your body. Furthermore, these tips will help you to stay active and bring the inflammation back to normal levels.

## 1. Stock Up Your Refrigerator and Pantry with Healthy Foods

To onboard the anti-inflammatory diet, you first have to fill up your home with healthy food items included in the diet. If your cabinets are full of junk and unhealthy eatables, you will be tempted to eat them.
However, if your fridge, cabinets, and pantry are stuffed with a healthy snack, then you'll reach for it and eat it. When you go grocery shopping, make sure to purchase lots of fruits, vegetables, yogurt, and nuts. So, that when you are looking for something to eat, you only find healthy options to snack on.

## 2. Swap Fizzy Drinks with Water

A tall glass of your favorite fizzy drink with fast food sounds quite yummy, doesn't it? But, fizzy drinks are loaded with sugar and other ingredients which are harmful to our bodies. The increased intake of fizzy drinks is associated with obesity, cholesterol, and Type-2 diabetes. Always carry a small water bottle when you are going out to drink water when thirsty. Do not indulge in sugary beverages.

## 3. Drink Black Coffee

Coffee helps lower down inflammation. But did you know adding sugar, cream, and other sweeteners to coffee can spike your blood sugar level and contribute to weight gain?
Instead of going for fancy and creamy coffees, stick to the old-school black coffee. It contains 0 calories and hence is an ideal beverage for restricting calories for weight loss.

## 4. Eat Mindfully

Whether you are having your main meals of the day or a simple snack time, make sure to focus only on your food. Watching TV or scrolling mobile distracts us from eating, and we end up eating more than our body requires.

Thus, eating mindfully will help you to understand when your body is full. It will prevent you from overstuffing yourself.

## 5. Add Green Tea to Your Diet

Just like plain black coffee or tea, green tea is also calorie-free. The light beverage is packed with rich antioxidants and flavonoids that reduce inflammation, flush toxins from the body, and suppress hunger at odd times.

## 6. Sleep Early

People do not consider a quality night of sleep essential for weight loss. During sleep, our body slows down and takes a rest. In case of poor or inadequate amount of sleep, our body feels lethargic. Due to that, people indulge in overeating.

When you are onboarding the anti-inflammatory diet, make sure that you don't forget about your sleep. Distant yourself from digital devices as they radiate the blue light. This light reduces melatonin, a hormone in our body that regulates our sleep. Create a comfortable environment and retire early to bed.

## 7. Plan Your Meals In Advanced

We understand that nobody likes to sweat in the kitchen to prepare food from scratch. When you are tired or have some friends over, ordering from a fast-food chain sounds like an amazing idea.

But, it can affect your diet and spike the inflammation levels in your body. Hence, always plan your meals and keep the refrigerator stocked with the required ingredients. For example, if you plan to make vegetable casseroles, chop and refrigerate the veggies in advance and grate the cheese. In this way, you feel less resistant to preparing your meals at home.

# 8. Indulge In Light Exercises

The primary reason why obesity is common in today's era is because of our sedentary lifestyle. People spend most of their sitting instead of moving or walking. This puts our body in the rest state, and it doesn't use the calories that we consume. As a result, the unused calories store themselves as fat, giving rise to plenty of other diseases.
An anti-inflammatory diet combined with regular exercises can speed up the healing process of inflammation, reduce unwanted weight, and prevent numerous diseases.

# Anti-Inflammatory Diet
# Breakfast Recipes

# 1. Challah Bread

**Preparation time**: 30 minutes

**Cooking time:** 25 minutes

**Servings:** 10 people

## Ingredients

- 2 ¼ teaspoon active dry yeast
- 1 cup warm water
- 4 cups all-purpose flour
- 7 eggs
- ¼ cup sugar
- 1 teaspoon salt
- 6 tablespoons extra virgin olive oil
- 2-3 tablespoon toasted sesame seeds

## Directions

1.  In a small bowl, combine the yeast with the warm water. Add a pinch of sugar. Stir to dissolve the yeast. Set aside until a foamy layer forms.
2.  Mix the flour, egg yolks, sugar, salt, and oil in a large bowl.
3.  Add the yeast mixture, and mix until too hard. Knead the dough for 10 minutes until soft and smooth.
4.  Place the dough in a lightly oiled mixing bowl. Cover with a kitchen cloth and keep it in a warm spot until the dough rises.
5.  Divide the dough into three equal pieces, then roll each piece into a rope. Braid the three ropes together.
6.  Cover and let it rise again (30 minutes). Meanwhile, preheat the oven to 350 F.
7.  Give it an egg wash. Sprinkle the sesame seeds.
8.  Bake for 20 minutes, until golden brown.

## Nutrition

- Calories: 124
- Carbohydrates: 22.2g

- Protein: 3.9g
- Fats: 6.5g
- Fiber: 0.9g

# 2. Baba Ganoush

**Preparation time**: 15 minutes
**Cooking time:** 20 minutes
**Servings:** 6 people

## Ingredients
- 2 Italian eggplants
- ¼ cup tahini paste
- 1 lemon
- 1 garlic clove (minced)
- 1 tablespoon Greek yogurt
- Kosher salt and black pepper
- 1 teaspoon sumac
- ¾ teaspoon pepper flakes
- Extra virgin olive oil
- Toasted pine nuts (garnishing)

## Directions
1. Place the eggplant directly over the flame. Turn the eggplant every 5 minutes until it is tender. The eggplant should deflate.
2. Remove the eggplant from the heat. Drain the excess water.
3. Peel the charred crispy skin off and discard it.
4. Transfer the eggplant to a bowl. Use a fork to break it down into smaller pieces.
5. Add the tahini paste, garlic, lemon juice, Greek yogurt, salt, pepper, sumac, pepper flakes.
6. Mix gently until well-combined.
7. Cover the baba ganoush and chill in the fridge for 30-60 minutes.
8. Transfer the baba ganoush to a rimmed serving dish. Top with extra virgin olive oil and toasted pine nuts. Serve with pita wedges!

## Nutrition

- Calories: 86.6
- Carbohydrates: 8.6g
- Protein: 3g
- Fats: 5.6g
- Fiber: 3.3g

# 3. Za'atar Olive Oil Fried Eggs

**Preparation time:** 1 minute
**Cooking time:** 2 minutes
**Servings:** 3 people

## Ingredients

- 3 eggs
- 3-6 tablespoon Extra virgin olive oil
- 0.75 teaspoon Kosher salt
- 6 teaspoon za'atar

## Directions

1. Over medium-high heat, warm a nonstick skillet. Add the olive oil and turn the heat to medium. Tilt the pan around to spread the oil.
2. Slide the eggs in the heated oil. Season with Kosher salt and the za'atar. Cook for about 2-3 minutes, spooning some olive oil on top until the egg is cooked.

## Nutrition

- Calories: 192.2
- Carbohydrates: 1.6g
- Protein: 5.7g

- Fats: 3.4g
- Fiber: 0.7g

# 4. Green Shakshuka

**Preparation time**: 10 minutes
**Cooking time:** 30 minutes
**Servings:** 4 people

## Ingredients

- ¼ cup Extra virgin olive oil
- 8 ounces' Brussels sprouts (sliced)
- Kosher salt
- ½ red onion
- 3 garlic cloves (minced)
- 1 bunch kale (8 ounces)
- 2 cups baby spinach (2.5 ounces)
- 1 teaspoon Aleppo pepper
- 1 teaspoon coriander
- ¾ teaspoon cumin
- ½ lemon
- 4 eggs
- 1 green onion
- Fresh parsley (garnishing)
- Crumbled feta (garnishing)

## Directions

1. In a skillet with a lid, heat the extra virgin olive oil until shimmering. Add the Brussels sprouts and sprinkle kosher salt. Cook for 5-6 minutes until soft.
2. Reduce the heat. Add onions and garlic, and cook for 3-4 minutes.

3. Add the kale and toss for 5 minutes. Add the spinach. Season with kosher salt.
4. Add the spices and ½ cup of water. Cover and cook for 8-10 minutes until completely wilted. Stir in the lemon juice.
5. Using a spoon, make 4 wells. Crack an egg into each well and season each egg with a bit of salt. Cover and cook for 4 minutes until the eggs have settled.
6. Remove from the heat. Garnish with green onions, parsley, and some feta. Serve with bread or warm pita.

## Nutrition

- Calories: 229.6
- Carbohydrates: 9.8g
- Protein: 9g
- Fats: 18.2g
- Fiber: 3g

# 5. Olive Oil Granola

**Preparation time**: 15 minutes
**Cooking time:** 40 minutes
**Servings:** 14 people

## Ingredients

- 2 ½ cups old fashioned rolled oats
- ¾ cup shelled pistachios
- ¾ cup walnuts
- ½ cup sunflower seed
- 3 tablespoons raw sesame seeds
- 1 cup unsweetened coconut flakes
- ¾ cup honey
- ½ cup Extra virgin olive oil
- 2 teaspoons pure vanilla extract
- ½ packed light brown sugar

- ½ teaspoon ground cinnamon
- ½ teaspoon cardamom
- ½ cup Medjool dates (pitted and chopped)
- ½ cranberries or cherries

## Directions

1. Preheat the oven to 350°F.
2. Combine the oats, pistachios, walnuts, sunflower seed, and sesame seeds, and coconut flakes in a large bowl.
3. In another bowl, mix the honey, olive oil, vanilla extract, brown sugar, cinnamon and cardamom. Pour over the oat mixture and toss until the oat mixture is well-coated.
4. Spread the mixture on a large sheet pan in one single layer. Bake in the heated oven, stirring every 7 to 10 minutes until the mixture is golden and well-toasted (anywhere from 30 to 45 minutes).
5. Remove from the heat and allow the granola to cool completely. Break it up into clusters and mix in the dates and cranberries (or other dried fruits of your choice)

## Nutrition

- Calories: 392kcal
- Carbohydrates: 40.1g
- Protein: 8.1g
- Fats: 1.6g
- Fiber: 5.4g

# Anti-Inflammatory Diet Lunch Recipes

# 6. Niçoise Salad

**Preparation time**: 20 minutes
**Cooking time:** 10 minutes
**Servings:** 5 people

## Ingredients
- 3-4 tomatoes (sliced)
- 4 ounces' soft lettuce
- 6 radishes (sliced)
- 1 cucumber (peeled)
- 1 cup Niçoise olives or black olives
- 1 cup artichoke hearts
- 4 hard-boiled eggs
- 1 5-ounce tuna
- 4 spring onions
- Black pepper
- 10 basil leaves
- 2 tablespoons red wine vinegar
- 2 tablespoons Dijon mustard
- Kosher salt
- 1/3 cup Extra virgin olive oil

## Directions
1. Put the tomato wedges in a large colander and place them over a bowl. Season the tomatoes with kosher salt and wait.
2. Top the lettuce with sliced radishes, cucumber, olives, artichoke heart quarters, eggs, and drained tomato wedges. Arrange chunks of tuna, green onions, and torn basil leaves all over. Sprinkle some black pepper.
3. For the dressing, mix tomato juice, red wine vinegar, Dijon mustard, and salt. Whisk to combine. Pour the olive oil until the dressing is emulsified.
4. Serve the dressing next to Nicoise salad.

## Nutrition

- Calories: 332.8

- Carbohydrates: 13.7g
- Protein: 9.8g
- Fats: 26.6g
- Fiber: 5.2g

# 7. Fish Piccata

**Preparation time**: 5 minutes
**Cooking time:** 15 minutes
**Servings:** 4 people

## Ingredients
- 1pound trout fillet
- Kosher salt and black pepper
- 1 teaspoon dried oregano
- 1 teaspoon paprika
- ¾ teaspoon garlic powder
- ¼ cup flour for dredging
- 1/3 cup Extra virgin olive oil
- 3 tablespoons unsalted butter
- 2 lemons (juice)
- ½ cup white wine
- 4 tablespoons capers
- Fresh chopped parsley

## Directions
1. Season the fish with salt and pepper. Mix the oregano, paprika, and garlic powder and season.
2. To dredge, coat the fish with flour. Gently shake excess flour.
3. In a large iron skillet, heat the olive oil and 2 tablespoons of unsalted butter over medium-high heat. Add the fish and cook for 2 to 3 minutes on each side until the fish is firm and flaky. Transfer the fish to a tray lined with a paper towel to drain excess oil.

4. To the same pan, add 1 more tablespoon of unsalted. Lower the heat, and add the lemon juice, white wine, and capers. Cook briefly over medium heat.
5. Return the fish to the pan and spoon the sauce over the fish.
6. Garnish with parsley and red pepper flakes.

## Nutrition

- Calories: 357.8
- Carbohydrates: 3.7g
- Protein: 25.5g
- Fats: 3.5g
- Fiber: 1.4g

# 8. Spanakorizo - Greek Spinach Rice

**Preparation time**: 20 minutes
**Cooking time:** 40 minutes
**Servings:** 4 people

## Ingredients
- 1 cup rice
- 4 tablespoons Extra virgin olive oil
- 1 yellow onion chopped
- 1pound baby spinach
- Juice of 1 lemon
- Kosher salt and black pepper
- 2 cloves garlic minced
- 2 tablespoons tomato paste
- 1 ½ teaspoon dried mint flakes
- 1 teaspoon dried dill weed
- Feta

## Directions

1. Rinse the rice. Put the rice in a bowl and add water to cover it by 1 inch. Soak for 20 minutes.
2. Heat ¼ cup extra virgin olive oil in a braising pan. Add the onions and cook for 5 minutes, until golden brown. Add the spinach, lemon juice, garlic, tomato paste, and a big pinch of kosher salt and black pepper. Sautee the spinach. Stir in the mint and dill weed.
3. Drain the rice and add it to the pan. Add 1 ½ cups of water. Boil it. Turn the heat to low.
4. Cook the rice for 20 minutes until dry.
5. Let the rice sit covered for 5-10 minutes.
6. Fluff the rice with a fork and garnish with feta and parsley.

## Nutrition

- Calories: 382.6
- Carbohydrates: 55.7g
- Protein: 7.9g
- Fats: 14.8g
- Fiber: 5.1g

# 9. Sheet Pan Chicken with Vegetables

**Preparation time**: 10 minutes
**Cooking time:** 20 minutes
**Servings:** 5 people

## Ingredients
- 2 medium zucchini
- 1 red pepper cored
- 1 red onion chopped
- 9 ounces' baby broccoli
- 1 ½ pound boneless chicken
- 5 garlic cloves, minced
- Kosher salt and black pepper
- 2 teaspoons oregano
- 1 teaspoon paprika
- 1 teaspoon coriander
- 1 lemon
- 1 teaspoon vinegar
- Extra virgin olive oil

## Directions
1. Preheat the oven to 400°F.
2. Place the veggies in a large bowl. Add chicken pieces and garlic. Season with kosher salt and black pepper. Add lemon juice, vinegar, and extra virgin olive oil. Toss it.
3. Transfer the chicken and vegetables to a large sheet pan.
4. Bake for 20 minutes.

## Nutrition

- Calories: 220.3kcal
- Carbohydrates: 13.4g
- Protein: 32.7g
- Fats: 4g
- Fiber: 3.4g

# 10. Egyptian Hawawshi

**Preparation time**: 15 minutes
**Cooking time:** 15 minutes
**Servings:** 4 people

## Ingredients
- 1 yellow onion
- 2 garlic cloves
- 1 green bell pepper chopped
- 1 jalapeno
- ½ ounce fresh parsley stems trimmed
- 2 pounds ground beef
- 3 tablespoons tomato paste
- Extra virgin olive oil
- 6 loaves pita bread

### For Seasoning
- 1 teaspoon coriander
- 1 teaspoon allspice
- 1 teaspoon paprika
- 1 teaspoon black pepper
- 1 teaspoon cumin
- ¾ teaspoon cardamom
- ¼ teaspoon cinnamon

## Directions
1. Preheat the oven to 400°F.
2. In a small bowl, add the spices and mix to combine.
3. Put the onion, garlic, bell pepper, jalapeno, and parsley in a food processor, pulse a few times until finely chopped. Transfer the mixture to a sieve to drain excess liquid.
4. Transfer the onion mixture to a large mixing bowl. Add the ground beef and tomato paste and mix. Add the spice mixture and kosher salt. Mix until the mixture is well combined.
5. Cut the pita loaves in halves to create 12 pita pockets.
6. Brush a large sheet pan with extra virgin olive oil.
7. Stuff each pita pocket with ⅓ cup of the meat mixture. Using the back of a spoon, spread the meat mixture inside the pita pockets.

8. Arrange the pitas in the prepared sheet pan. Brush the pita pocket tops with a bit of extra virgin olive oil.
9. Bake in the heated oven for 15 minutes, then carefully turn the pitas over and cook on the other side another 5-10 minutes until the meat is fully cooked and the pita is crispy.

## Nutrition

- Calories: 204.8
- Carbohydrates: 2.9g
- Protein: 13.5g
- Fats: 5.8g
- Fiber: 0.8g

# Anti-Inflammatory Diet Dinner Recipes

# 11. Falafel

**Preparation time:** 15 minutes
**Cooking time:** 35 minutes
**Servings:** 4 people

## Ingredients
- 2 cups chickpeas
- ½ teaspoon baking soda
- 1 cup parsley leaves
- ¾ cup cilantro leaves
- ½ cup dill
- 1 onion
- 7-8 garlic cloves
- Salt
- 1 tablespoon black pepper
- 1 tablespoon cumin
- 1 tablespoon coriander
- 1 teaspoon baking powder
- 2 tablespoons roasted sesame seeds
- Oil
- Falafel (Tahini) sauce

## Directions
1. Place the chickpeas and baking soda in a large bowl filled with water to cover 2 inches. Soak overnight for 18 hours. Now drain the chickpeas completely and pat them dry.
2. Add the chickpeas, herbs, onions, garlic, and spices to a food processor. Run the food processor 40 seconds at a time to form a mixture.
3. Transfer the falafel mixture to a container and cover tightly. Refrigerate for 1 hour.
4. Just before frying, add the baking powder and sesame seeds to the mixture and stir with a spoon.
5. Scoop tablespoonful of the falafel mixture and form into patties (have wet hands).
6. Fill a medium saucepan with oil. Heat on medium-high. Fry the patties for 3-5 minutes until crispy.
7. Assemble the falafel patties in pita bread with tahini or hummus, arugula, tomato, and cucumbers.

## Nutrition

- Calories: 93kcal
- Carbohydrates: .4g
- Protein: 3.9g
- Fats: 3.8g
- Fiber: 2g

# 12. Lentils and Rice with Crispy Onions

**Preparation time**: 20 minutes
**Cooking time:** 50 minutes
**Servings:** 5 people

## Ingredients
- 1 cup black lentils
- 4 cups water
- ¼ cup Extra virgin olive oil
- 2 yellow onions
- Kosher salt
- 1 cup rice (soaked)
- Black pepper
- Parsley

## Directions
1. Place the lentils in a small saucepan with 2 cups of water. Boil for 10-12 minutes. Remove from the heat, drain the lentils.
2. In a large sauté pan, heat the oil. Add the diced onions and cook for about 40 minutes; sprinkle the onions with a teaspoon of salt.
3. Pour 2 cups of water, boil for 2 minutes. Stir the rice and par-cooked lentils into the onion mixture.

4. Cover and boil. Add a pinch of salt and pepper. Reduce the heat and cook until rice and lentils are cooked through. Remove from the heat and season with salt and pepper. Serve the Mujadara with parsley garnish.
5. Fry the onions until golden brown. Arrange them on top of the Mujadara.

## Nutrition

- Calories: 405
- Carbohydrates: 52.4g
- Protein: 10.9g
- Fats: 2.4g
- Fiber: 2.5g

# 13. Sweet Potato Stew

**Preparation time**: 10 minutes
**Cooking time:** 35 minutes
**Servings:** 6 people

## Ingredients

- 1 teaspoon ground coriander
- 1 teaspoon ground cumin
- ¾ teaspoon Aleppo pepper
- ½ teaspoon turmeric
- Extra virgin olive oil
- 1 yellow onion chopped
- 4 garlic cloves minced
- 3 carrots chopped
- 3 sweet potatoes 1pound
- Kosher Salt and black pepper
- 1 15-ounces diced tomatoes
- 3 cups vegetable broth

- 5 ounces baby spinach
- 1 cup fresh parsley

## Directions

1. In a small bowl, add the spices (coriander, cumin, Aleppo pepper, and turmeric). Mix to combine.
2. In a large heavy pot, heat 2 tablespoon extra-virgin olive oil over medium heat until shimmering. Add onions and garlic and cook for 3 minutes, stirring occasionally.
3. Add carrots and sweet potatoes. Season with kosher salt, black pepper, and the spice mixture. Raise the heat to medium-high, and cook, stirring occasionally, for about 4 to 5 minutes.
4. Add tomatoes and broth. Boil for 10 minutes, then turn the heat to low. Cover the pot only part-way, allowing an opening at the top for the stew to "breath." Cook for about 20 to 25 minutes, or until sweet potatoes are fully cooked and tender.
5. Finally, stir in the baby spinach and fresh parsley. Remove from heat, and finish with a generous drizzle of extra virgin olive oil. Serve over quick-cooked couscous. Enjoy!

## Nutrition

- Calories: 128
- Carbohydrates: 24.3g
- Protein: 3.4g
- Fats: 0.5g
- Fiber: 4.6g

# 14. Foul Mudammas

**Preparation time**: 15 minutes
**Cooking time:** 10 minutes
**Servings:** 5 people

## Ingredients
- 2 cans fava beans
- ½ cup water
- Kosher salt
- 1 teaspoon cumin
- 2 jalapenos
- 2 garlic cloves
- 1 lemon
- Extra virgin olive oil
- Parsley
- 1 tomato
- Tomatoes
- Cucumbers
- Green onions
- Olives
- Pita bread

## Directions
1. In a skillet or saucepan, add the fava beans and ½ cup water. Warm over medium heat. Sprinkle with kosher salt and cumin. Mash the fava beans.
2. Smash the hot peppers and garlic. Add lemon juice and stir to form the sauce.
3. Pour the sauce over fava beans. Add extra virgin olive oil. Top with parsley.
4. Serve with pita bread, sliced veggies, and olives.

## Nutrition

- Calories: 154
- Carbohydrates: 22.3g
- Protein: 0.9g
- Fats: 3.5g
- Fiber: 1.8g

# 15. Vegetarian Pasta Faggioli

**Preparation Time**: 15 Minutes
**Cooking Time:** 15 Minutes
**Servings:** 6 People

## Ingredients
- 8 ounces' small pasta
- Extra virgin olive oil
- 1 yellow onion chopped
- 2 celery stalks chopped
- 2 carrots chopped
- 2 garlic cloves chopped
- 1 bay leaf
- 1 teaspoon oregano
- 1 28-ounces' can fire roasted tomatoes
- 5-6 cups vegetable broth
- 1 15-ounces can beans
- Salt and pepper
- ½ cup basil leaves
- Parmesan cheese

## Directions
1. In a boiling pot of water, cook the pasta. Drain well, and set aside.
2. In an iron pot, heat 2 tablespoon olive oil. Sauté the onions, celery and carrots on medium heat for 4 minutes or so until the vegetables begin to break down. Add garlic, bay leaf, and dried oregano. Cook for another 2 minutes, stirring occasionally.
3. Now, add the roasted diced tomatoes, vegetable broth, cannellini beans, and beans. Season with salt and pepper to taste. Boil, then reduce the heat to simmer. Cover the pot with a lid but leave a small opening. Simmer for 10-15 minutes.
4. Bring to a medium-high heat, stir in the pasta until warmed through. Stir in the fresh basil, and remove from heat.
5. In your mixing bowl, whisk together the eggs, baking powder, milk, feta, parsley, thyme, and a pinch of kosher salt and black pepper. Fold in the roasted vegetables.
6. Transfer to serving bowls and top with crushed red pepper (optional) and grated Parmesan cheese. Add your favorite crusty Italian bread. Enjoy!

## Nutrition

- Calories: 445
- Carbohydrates: 80.4g
- Protein: 20.3g
- Fats: 0.6g
- Fiber: 14.7g

# INTERMITTENT FASTING

# METHOD TO MIX UP

# Chapter 1. What is Intermittent Fasting?

Maintaining a healthy weight and leading an active lifestyle is an uphill task in today's era. We are surrounded by technology throughout the day. TV, the internet, mobile applications, and social media have limited our activities and movements.

Less physical activities and unhealthy eating habits lead our body to pile up unhealthy weight. This, in return, results in many harmful diseases such as cholesterol, high blood pressure, and even diabetes.

Plenty of fad diets are available on the internet to burn excess weight. These diets may shed fat, but they are not effective in the long run. If you truly want to lose weight and maintain a healthy lifestyle, you must switch to a healthy lifestyle. And intermittent fasting will prove to your best friend towards a healthy and active body.

You must have seen many people praising intermittent fasting and how it transformed their bodies. Believe those people because intermittent fasting has the power to reduce your body fat, detox your body, and help you get rid of many diseases.

Intermittent fasting focuses on the eating pattern. It provides a timeframe for eating and fasting for a certain number of hours. Unlike many diets, intermittent fasting doesn't specify what to eat; rather, its main focus is on '*when to eat.*'

The most common method of intermittent fasting is fasting for 16 hours and eating during the 8-hour window. During the fasting window, you can consume water and non-calorie beverages. Your body shouldn't get any food or calorie-based beverages. As it will start using the calories to run the important body functions.

Intermittent fasting is hyped up for a reason. Because the body burns the stubborn fast as energy, which results in weight loss without following any fad diet.

Let's have a look at how intermittent fasting works.

# How Does Intermittent Fasting Work?

When our body goes without food for several hours, metabolic switching occurs inside the body. When fasting, he doesn't eat his meals or snacks to generate energy. Instead, the body starts to exhaust the sugar and fat stores for energy.

Normally, our body doesn't use fat stores. It relies on the food we eat for energy. The body turns the food into fuel. It carries out the important functions and stores the remaining or unused energy as fat reserves in our body. When the fat percentage in our body increases, it leads to weight gain.

During intermittent fasting, the body has to keep functioning and generate energy. Therefore, it uses up the stored fat as energy. This, in return, burns the fat and results in weight loss.

There are many ways to start intermittent fasting. The following chapter will cover the basic intermittent fasting plans.

# Chapter 2. Why Is Intermittent Fasting Important For Women?

For females who have an interest in weight loss, intermittent fasting may resemble a great choice; however, great deals of people would like to know, should women fast? Is Intermittent fasting reliable for females? There have been a couple of essential study studies about intermittent fasting, which can assist in losing some weight on this intriguing new nutritional trend.

Intermittent fasting is likewise called alternate-day fasting, although there are absolutely some variants on this diet plan. The American Journal of Clinical Nutrition did a research study just recently that enlisted 16 overweight guys and ladies on a 10-week program. Individuals absorbed food to 25% of their approximated power requirements on the fasting days. They got dietary coaching the rest of the time; nonetheless, they were not provided a particular criterion to adhere to throughout this moment.

What made this a fascinating exploration was that many individuals need to lose even more weight than these researchers before seeing the same adjustments. It was a fantastic discovery that has spurred a great number of individuals to try fasting.

Intermittent fasting for ladies has some beneficial results. Women that are following a healthy diet and workout strategy might be having a problem with persistent fat. However, fasting is a reasonable solution to this.

## Intermittent Fasting for Women Over 50

Undoubtedly, our bodies and our metabolic rate changes when we get to menopause. One of the most substantial modifications that ladies over 50 experience is that they have a slower metabolic process and begin to gain weight. Fasting may be an exceptional way to avoid this weight and also turn around the gain. Study research studies have shown that this fasting pattern assists in controlling hunger. Also, individuals who follow it regularly do not experience the same yearnings as others do. Suppose you're over 50 and attempting to change to your slower metabolic process. In that case, recurring fasting can help you stop consuming too much daily.

Your body also begins to establish some chronic conditions like high cholesterol and high blood pressure when you reach 50. Periodic fasting has been exposed to reduce both cholesterol and blood stress, even without a fantastic offer of weight reduction. Suppose you've begun to observe your numbers enhancing at the doctor's work environment yearly. In that case, you may be able to bring them back down with fasting and without shedding much weight.

Recurring fasting may not be an exceptional idea for every solitary woman. Anybody with a specific health condition or that often tends to be a hypoglycemic need to speak with a physician. This new dietary pattern has certain benefits for females who naturally store more fat in their bodies and could have a problem doing away with these fat deposits.

# Chapter 3. Intermittent Fasting For Women Over 50 and Its Detailed Importance

According to research, an intermittent fasting diet does more than just burn fat. This metabolic change affects your brain and body. There are numerous health benefits of practicing intermittent fasting, including long and healthy life, a sharp mind, and a lean body. Many changes happen when intermittent fasting, which protects your organs from chronic diseases such as heart disease, type 2 diabetes, some neurodegenerative disorders, many cancers, and inflammatory diseases. Different variations in intermittent fasting diet plans show pretty fantastic health benefits.

Research has backed this belief that it might have various positive effects, ranging from weight loss and a healthier body to a low risk of numerous diseases and a prolonged lifespan. But, fasting usually is not advisable for children, people having severe health issues, and pregnant women. Here are given some amazing benefits of intermittent fasting that research has approved so far:

## Improvement in Brain and Memory Function

According to research, intermittent fasting helps boost memory performance in animals and adult humans. This eating pattern also improves brain function. It helps in combating diseases like Alzheimer's. As per another study, intermittent fasting also enhances cognitive function, neuroplasticity, which structures the ability of your brain to rebuild and reorganize itself, and the overall improvement in the brain functions.

## Better Endurance Level

Intermittent fasting maintains muscle mass and helps in fat loss. It enhances endurance levels and improves physical performance. Research done on mice has shown positive outcomes in these aspects. The growth hormone also shows increased levels as a result of intermittent fasting. Which ultimately helps in improving body composition and metabolism. It also improves the health of our tissues in the long term.

## Control Diabetes

Adult humans with obesity can lose weight by adopting an effective intermittent fasting plan that ultimately controls diabetes as it helps significantly decrease and control the levels of blood sugar. In recent times, intermittent fasting has become novel and one of the most effective ways to treat type 2, diabetes patients. There are many reports of cases where patients lost weight and witnessed improved blood sugar levels. They did not have to take diabetes medications, and the disease appeared less harmful. But more research is needed to prove this approach as safe and useful in the long term as intermittent fasting demands a significant change in eating habits. Not many people can stick to that in the long term.

## Improved Heart Health

The positive changes in intermittent fasting lower cholesterol levels. Intermittent fasting improves blood pressure. It maintains and keeps the heart rate in balance. It keeps the risk factors in control that may cause heart-related issues and disease. According to the studies, when the insulin levels in your blood fall, the risk of serious cardiovascular events like heart failure will also fall. It is crucial for type 2 diabetes patients. These patients are at risk of heart diseases 2-4 times more than people without diabetes. Observational research has shown that intermittent fasting delivers both metabolic and cardiovascular benefits. It is noteworthy that changes in metabolic parameters like lower blood sugar and triglycerides happen because of weight loss, and intermittent fasting can help you achieve that.

## Decrease Inflammation

Research has found that intermittent fasting patterns reduce certain blood markers that can cause inflammation. According to research, intermittent fasting kick-start releases monocytes, immune cells related to high inflammation that can lead to severe damage to the tissues. Its population has been increasing the body's blood circulation because of unhealthy eating habits people have adopted in recent years. These cells usually go into sleep mode in fasting periods. They become less inflammatory in their effects than those cells fed. According to researchers, monocytes significantly decrease in numbers after fasting, which is the strong link between inflammatory disease and high-calorie diet patterns. Considering the number of illnesses caused by chronic inflammation, there should be an enormous investigation of the effects of fasting on anti-inflammation because many people are being affected by this.

## Effective in Cancer Treatment

Although there has not been much research on the possible relationship between intermittent fasting and cancer, early reports suggest positive results. The study conducted on cancer patients has suggested that the consequences of chemotherapy might be eliminated by having a fast before treatment. It has also been supported by other studies where the cancer patients had the alternate day fast. Their fasting approach before chemotherapy treatment resulted in positive cure rates. So, the comprehensive analysis of cancer and fasting has supported the argument that fasting reduces cancer risk and various cardiovascular diseases.

Intermittent fasting has considerable potential for prevention and also the treatment of cancer. As we know, intermittent fasting reduces glucose and insulin levels. It increases Ketone body and anti- inflammatory levels, generating a large protective environment to reduce carcinogenesis and DNA damage. Thus, intermittent fasting not only protects you from cancer but also enhances the natural death of the pre-cancerous damaging cells. A study conducted on ten subjects having various malignancies showed that combining fasting with chemotherapy showed a decrease in commonly seen side effects of chemotherapy. The impact of fasting on the toxicity of chemotherapy and cancer progression is being studied in various clinical researches in the US and Europe.

## Weight-Loss

Most people trying intermittent fasting have gained positive results in cutting their weight. You may plan heavy meals, but eating them consistently is not an easy practice. Intermittent fasting is a useful option for someone looking forward to weight loss as it provides the most amazing and simple way to lose the overall calories without even changing your lifestyle that much. Also, if someone eats large portions for lunch and the evening meal, they will have fewer calorie intake than someone who has 3-4 regular meals. Cutting out meals in intermittent fasting works very well for losing weight.

When you try to decrease calorie intake, losing weight is inevitable dramatically. But it will not do any good for you. It will cause many health problems for you, including severe muscle loss. When you go for intermittent fasting, the body moves towards a conservation mode that burns calories lowly. It is not the Fat: the body burns at the early stages of fasting; it is the water or fluid. When you turn back to the eating period, any lost weight will return quickly. Most people tend to regain the weight that they lost during fasting. They possibly add extra lbs. just because gaining weight happens because of slower metabolism. So, it is crucial to practice the right approach and choose the one that goes for Fat: burning and more effective weight loss.

## Detoxify Your Body

Intermittent fasting might be a stressful activity, and your body might take time to adjust to it. It might not immediately love the idea, but it will ultimately give you huge benefits. According to research, even an occasional fast has a lot of benefits, and it has been proven with research that autophagy and intermittent fasting can cure cancer. It can make the treatment more productive and protect healthy cells while reducing the side effects of the treatment. The resting period involved in intermittent fasting enhances autophagy, a crucial function of your body to detoxify and clean out the dead and damaged cells. Giving your body a small break in digestion and constant eating gives it a better place to heal itself. It helps eliminate all the junk inside your body cells that might accelerate the aging process. A study found out that time-limited feeding, as we do in intermittent fasting, increases the expression of an autophagy gene and a protein called mTOR that regulates cell growth. It has been done on 11 participants for four consecutive days. Another study has shown that food limitation is a very well-recognized approach to boost autophagy that offers many protective benefits to your brain.

Training your body for autophagy will benefit you in the very long term. Autophagy refers to self- eating your body. It might sound scary, but it is one of the effective ways to cleanse the body. So, your body itself becomes your cleansing house. During this process, cells create many membranes to hunt down dead scraps or diseased cells. Then it strips them into parts and utilizes the molecules to gain energy. It can also help make a new cell. It is your body ˀ s recycling program. Research has shown that autophagy plays a

119

role in the immune response and inflammation. It acts as a perfect immune effector that mediates pathogen clearance.

Autophagy is the phenomenon of self-digestion that happens inside your body cells during intermittent fasting periods. It controls essential physiological functions that break down cellular components and then recycles them. Autophagy rapidly provides fuel to gain energy. It serves as a very strong base that leads to the renewal of the cellular components. Therefore, it plays a crucial part in cellular response and controls starvation and stress during fasting periods.

Autophagy eliminates invading intracellular viruses and bacteria. That is how it cleans your body. Your body cells use autophagy for the elimination of damaged organelles and proteins. Through this mechanism, it counterattacks the negative results of aging.

## Metabolic Syndrome and Intermittent Fasting

Intermittent fasting can reverse many metabolic syndromes by enhancing insulin sensitivity, balancing blood pressure, and stimulating lipolysis. Reduced body fat, balanced blood pressure, and glucose metabolism are some of the additional benefits of intermittent fasting. The research done on obese people in which they were studied for 6 months while on an intermittent fasting diet, consuming only 500–600 calorie intakes during fasting periods, showed an abdominal fat loss, improved sensitivity levels of insulin, and blood pressure.

## Anti-Aging

You will not find a lot of research on human bodies regarding intermittent fasting. Although some research done on animals suggests that it boosts lifespan and slows down the aging signs. Calorie restriction is the best and the most effective approach to combat aging. The traditional calorie restriction cuts down the calories by almost 20–40%, which is not the best option, and plan to do things that way. The recent research on animals and humans has shown many previously unknown mechanisms involved in anti-aging. There are some additional effects of intermittent fasting on human cells, which lead to the potential anti-aging phenomenon. It includes the mTOR pathway, ketogenesis, and autophagy.

Choosing intermittent fasting without suffering from malnutrition is the most consistent and efficient anti-aging intervention. It unquestionably expands lifespan according to the research done on animals and some humans. The study found that the longevity biomarkers, i.e., insulin level and body temperature, and DNA damage lessened significantly in humans by extended intermittent fasting. Other mechanisms also prove the claim made by researchers in explaining the anti-aging effects by adopting intermittent fasting, including decreased lipid peroxidation, high efficiency of the oxidative repair, increased antioxidant defense system, and reduced mitochondrial generation rate.

## Low-Calorie Intake in an Efficient Way

Following an approach like 16/8 intermittent fasting, you eat for just 8-hour a day. It helps in limiting the calorie intake level. Typically, people have more calorie intake than what is actually needed. One of the most efficient habits to remain healthy and stop fats from growing significantly in the body is by adopting the habit of exercising 4-5 days every week. It burns extra calories in the body. People eating many fast foods take more calories and unhealthy nutrients in their diet. But intermittent fasting protects your body from storing that extra Fat: having less calorie intake in the body.

# Chapter 4. Intermittent Fasting for Women for Over 40-60

If you are a woman of 50 years or more and do not know what to do to lose weight, here we bring you the solution. We show you a diet based on the number of calories you should consume according to your age.

It is recommended to consume around 1,500 calories per day. However, 1,200 calories per day are recommended if you are a sedentary woman. Remember that lack of physical activity increases the chances of gaining weight considerably.

The parts where fat is most concentrated are in the hips, legs, and abdomen. Hormonal changes affect the body considerably. For this reason, for women of this age, their metabolism is slower, increasing the chances of gaining weight.

In general, the diet required   includes:

1. Fruits, vegetables, and legumes. The best source of protein is that which does not provide much fat, such as fish, chicken, turkey, and nuts.
2. You should eat fat very sparingly whenever they come from a healthy source, such as olive oil.
3. To maintain strong bones, you must take at least 1,200 mg. calcium a day. You can take it from food or take it as a supplement.

# Main Sources of Micronutrients

- With regard to dairy products, it is advisable to drink 1-2 glasses of skim milk or yogurt a day. 1 c. yogurt contains about the same amount of calcium as 1 c. milk.
- It is also advisable to eat around 50 g. fresh cheese.

- A sufficient amount of vitamin D is also needed to metabolize calcium, and women over 70 have to take a recommended daily dose of 800 IU. Sunlight helps get vitamin D, as do some foods, such as:
  o Egg yolks
  o The cheese
  o Fortified dairy products.
  o Ask your doctor if a vitamin D supplement might be helpful.

In addition to this, it is recommended to take 2 ½ c. vegetables a day. The more varied, the better. The diet of older women should be rich in fiber for the gastrointestinal organs to function properly and avoid problems such as constipation.

Low carbohydrate and protein-rich diets are not very advisable for senior women, as they can cause metabolic problems.

It is best to eat mainly polyunsaturated and monounsaturated fat like the one that comes from olive oil. Although you should not consume more than the equivalent of 5-6 tbsp. Oil a day.

Physical activity is good for burning the calories ingested, preventing weight gain. This does not mean that older people have to sign up for a gym or run a marathon.

# The Changes Women Over 50 Are Bound to Face and How to Approach This Nutritionally

## 1. Mood and Insomnia during Menopause

It is common to suffer moodiness during this period of a woman 's life. This can negatively affect the moment of making decisions that affect our health care. In addition, this stage can be aggravated if you have insomnia. Although they have no solution, both situations can be approached from the nutritional point of view. How? Eating foods that produce emotional well-being, relaxation, and increase serotonin production. For example, dark chocolate, hot milk with cinnamon, banana, or nuts.

## 2. Lack of Energy

Feeling tired is also frequent at this stage. That is why it is important to follow a well-planned diet, with small but constant intakes throughout the day. For example, distributed in 5–7 meals. Also, avoid foods that can worsen the feeling of lack of energy, such as sugars and stimulant drinks. Sugars give energy quickly but produce an on-off effect that produces a subsequent sugar downturn. Stimulating drinks such as coffee or tea should not be avoided but controlled since they make the rest worse and cause us to be more tired and lack energy.

## 3. Bone Decalcification When Menstruation Disappears

Estrogens have a protective effect on bone tissue. When the woman ' s body stops producing them, alterations in the regulation of calcium are triggered, causing a loss of bone mass. At the nutritional level, we must avoid bone loss with 3 main factors:
- Calcium intake through milk, yogurt, almonds, orange, broccoli, cabbage.
- Minimizing the intake of salt favors the elimination of calcium through the urine.
- Ensuring a good supply of exogenous vitamin D (food and/ or supplementation) and endogenous (the body itself manufactured with sun exposure).
- In addition to minimizing decalcifying products such as sugar and carbonated drinks.

## 4. Cardiovascular Risk

124

From menopause, the risk of cardiovascular diseases increases. Normally cholesterol tends to rise. We recommend doing a heart-healthy diet by increasing the intake of healthy fats (extra virgin oil, nuts, and avocado) and avoiding saturated fats (cheeses, sausages) and Trans fats (processed foods such as chips, cereal bars, and cookies).

## 5. Weight Gain and Redistribution of Body Fat

The change that stands out and annoys, physically speaking, upon reaching menopause is weight gain. In this stage of life, fat stops accumulating mostly in the hips and is placed in greater amounts in the belly or abdomen. This is also one factor that increases cardiovascular risk, cholesterol, and blood pressure. This means that we will probably have to watch more what we eat and perhaps do a hypocaloric diet.

## 6. Loss of Muscle Mass

In the case weight gain is not enough, this increase is accompanied in addition to a decrease in muscles. This change is inevitable, but we must face it with a diet rich in lean proteins (rabbit, turkey, white fish) and with the physical exercise of strength or toning.

## 7. Changes in Food Preferences

Finally, it is worth highlighting some common changes in women's diet from menopause due to new food preferences or root diets and attempts to lose weight. This is usually reflected in dinners, which become a yogurt or a salad or a piece of bread. This can worsen weight gain and loss of muscle mass due to a lack of Protein: and cooked vegetables.

## 8. Fluid Retention

Hormonal changes that occur in menopause can cause fluid retention. This factor does not affect all women equally. In the same way that women retain fluids with menstruation and others who do not, it happens the same at this stage. Changes in estrogen levels affect the body's water balance. How to combat fluid retention? Consuming little salt, boosting vegetables rich in Fiber: and antioxidants, drinking a high amount of water, and doing physical exercise.

During menopause, combat fluid retention by consuming little salt, fiber-rich vegetables, and antioxidants. Do not forget to drink a lot of water and exercise.

# Slimming by Age: From 30—50 Years Old

## *Why Do You Gain Weight?*

During this stage of life, many things happen: life as a couple, postpartum, professional changes, moving. If you have children and work, you will know that the time and the desire to cook are practically null, so sometimes tends to carelessness about healthy eating.

## *How to Lead a More Balanced Life*

**Eat moderately:** Do not overdo dinner. It is usually when we get out of control: we arrive home after working all day and do not measure the amount of food.

**Share in moderation:** Be careful at snack time with children. You can eat a slice of whole wheat bread with some fruit, 100% natural peanut butter, and some nuts. Just like your children! It is best to avoid processed products, both for them and you.

## *Weight-Loss Menu According to This Age Range*

The menu proposed

**Breakfast:** 1 plain yogurt or 150 ml. semi-skim milk; 60 g. bread or 1c. Croissant; 10 g. butter or margarine; 1 c. jam coffee.

**Lunch:** 40 g. natural tuna or 1egg or 50 g. sausage; 150 g. raw and/ or cooked vegetables; 150 g. cooked starches (50 g. raw); 10 ml. olive oil (2 c. coffee); 1plain yogurt; 1 fruit or 1 sweet.

**Dinner:** 250 ml. vegetable soup or 100 g. vegetables; 150 g. cooked potato (50 g. raw); 10 g. (2 c. coffee) olive oil; 150 g. cooked fish or 130 g. cooked meat/ chicken; 40 g. bread; 1fruit or 2 ice cream balls.

# Slimming By Age: At 50 Years Old and above

## *Why Do You Gain Weight?*

One of the major hormonal changes in the life of women with the arrival of menopause is approaching. And this change in the body usually has consequences on the figure. The appetite can increase, the fat tends to accumulate and be located especially in the abdomen. More liquids can be retained than before.

## *How to Lead a More Balanced Life*

**Resume or increase your sports activity:** Your basic metabolism tends to decrease. To compensate for it, it is necessary to increase energy expenditure with activities that prevent the accumulation of fat walking, running, cycling, Pilates, yoga, stretching.

**Make a snack:** To avoid itching between hours anarchistically, it is best to make an afternoon snack based on whole wheat bread or oatmeal to calm the appetite. If you are hungry, choose a fruit, a natural yogurt, nuts, or chocolate (more than 70% always).

**Organize your little whims:** To not feel frustrated after a meal, it is best to cook scrumptious recipes to avoid monotony and better control what you eat. You can also add, without abusing, some foods that you like to give yourself a whim from time to time.

## *Weight-Loss Menu According to This Age*

Proposed menu:
**Breakfast:** 50 ml. semi-skim milk; 60 g. bread; 8 g. butter or margarine and 2 c. jam coffee; 1 fruit.

**Lunch:** 150 g. cooked starches; 1 plate of raw or cooked vegetables; 100 g. cooked Meat/ chicken; 2 c. oil coffee; 1 plain yogurt; 1 fruit Snack: 60 g. bread; 40 g. cheese or 30 g. Chocolate.

**Dinner:** 1 plate of vegetable soup or 200 g. raw/ cooked vegetables; 80 g. cooked fish or 1 slice of cooked ham or 50 g. sausage; 1c. Oil coffee; 1 plain yogurt; 1 fruit.
Do not forget, in general, to vary foods during the week. It is very important to eat legumes or exercise frequently

# Chapter5. 14-Day Diet Plan Intermittent Fasting for Women 50

| DAY | BREAKFAST | LUNCH | DINNER |
|---|---|---|---|
| 1. | Chia Breakfast Bowl | Tilapia Delight | Mushroom Pork Chops |
| 2. | Special Intermittent Bread | Intermittent Lasagna | Broccoli Rice With Mushrooms |
| 3. | Breakfast Cereal | Pork Burrito Bowl | Cucumber Avocado Salad With Bacon |
| 4. | Baked Omelet With Bacon | Steamed Artichokes | Spicy Intermittent Chicken Wings |
| 5. | Eggs and Bell peppers | Salmon and Tomatoes | Salsa Chicken Bites |
| 6. | Delicious Flax Pancakes | Tuna Casserole | Pesto Pork Chops |
| 7. | Sausage and Veggies Frittata | Stuffed Chicken Breasts | Lemonade Broccoli |
| 8. | Eggs in Avocado Boat | Pork Stir-Fry | Mexican Cod Fillets |
| 9. | Cherry Tomatoes Omelet | Herb Pesto Tuna | Tamari Steak Salad |
| 10. | Cream Cheese Soufflé | Italian Chicken With Asparagus and Artichoke Hearts | Vegetable en Papillote |
| 11. | Sausage Quiche | Chives Trout | Blackened Chicken |
| 12. | Breakfast Frittata | Cheesy Chicken and Mushroom Casserole | Roasted Red pepper and Eggplant Soup |
| 13. | Turkey and Scrambled eggs Breakfast | Tilapia and Red Sauce | Buffalo Pizza Chicken |
| 14. | Intermittent Waffles | Beef Stroganoff With Protein Noodles | Buttery Scallops |

# 200 Recipes to insert in your personal meal plan

## ANTI INFLAMMATORY DIET AND MEDITERRANEAN DIET
### Mixed up with Intermittent Fasting

# Breakfast

## 1. Breakfast Frittata

**Preparation time:** 10 minutes

**Cooking time:** 30 minutes

**Servings:** 2

## Ingredients

- 2 eggs, beaten
- 2 tbsps. liquid egg whites
- 2 tbsps. whole Ricotta cheese
- Pinch sea salt
- Pinch ground mustard spice
- Pinch black pepper
- ¼ c. fresh spinach, chopped
- 2 slices bacon, cooked and crumbled
- 2 slices tomato
- 2 tbsps. grated cheese

## Directions

1. Preheat the oven to 400°F. Grease a pie dish.
2. In a bowl, combine beaten eggs, egg whites, Ricotta, sea salt, mustard, and black pepper. Whisk and beat well.
3. Add the crumbled bacon and spinach to the mixture and mix.
4. Pour the egg mixture into the prepared pie dish. Place the tomato slices on top.
5. Bake for 30 minutes.
6. Remove from the oven and sprinkle with cheese.
7. Cool, slice, and serve.

## Nutrition

- Calories: 116
- Fat: 9 g.
- Carb: 1 g.
- Protein: 0 g.

- 

## 2. Intermittent Waffles

**Preparation time:** 5 minutes

**Cooking time:** 10 minutes

**Servings:** 2

## Ingredients

- ¼ c. almond milk, unsweetened
- ¼ tsp. apple cider vinegar
- 1 egg
- ½ tbsp. olive oil
- ¼ tsp. vanilla extract
- ½ c. almond flour
- 1 tbsp. coconut flour
- 1 tsp. baking powder
- 1 tsp. Erythritol

## Directions

1. Preheat the waffle iron and grease it.
2. In a bowl, mix apple cider vinegar and almond milk.
3. Add vanilla extract, olive oil, and egg to this mixture. Whisk to combine and set aside.
4. In another bowl, combine baking powder, coconut flour, almond flour, and Erythritol. Whisk the dry ingredients together.
5. Combine the dry flour mixture with the wet mixture and whisk to mix.
6. Pour about ¼ c. batter in the waffle iron.
7. Cook about three to five minutes until steam stops rising from the waffle iron.
8. Repeat and serve.

135

## Nutrition

- Calories: 211
- Fat: 16 g.
- Carb: 6.5 g.
- Protein: 8 g.

# 3. Ricotta Omelet With Swiss Chard

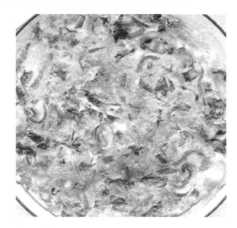

**Preparation time:** 10 minutes

**Cooking time:** 15 minutes

**Servings:** 2

## Ingredients

- 6 eggs
- 2 tbsps. almond milk
- ½ tsp. kosher salt
- ½ tsp. ground black pepper
- 6 tbsps. unsalted butter, divided
- 2 bunch Swiss chard, cleaned and stemmed
- ⅔ c. Ricotta

## Directions

1. Add the eggs and milk. Season with salt and pepper then whisk. Set aside.
2. In a skillet, melt 4 tbsps. butter. Add the veggie leaves and sauté until just wilted. Remove from pan. Set aside.
3. Now melt 1 tbsp. butter in the skillet.
4. Add ½ the egg mixture. Spread the mixture. Cook for about 2 minutes.
5. Add ½ the Ricotta when the edges are firm, but the center is still a bit runny.
6. Bend ⅓ the omelet over the Ricotta filling. Transfer to a plate.
7. Repeat with the remaining butter and egg mixture.
8. Serve with Swiss chard.

## Nutrition

- Calories: 693
- Fat: 60 g.
- Carb: 8 g.
- Protein: 2 g.

# 4. Omelet With Goat Cheese and Herb

**Preparation time:** 5 minutes

**Cooking time:** 12 minutes

**Servings:** 2

## Ingredients

- 6 eggs, beaten
- 2 tbsps. chopped herbs (basil, parsley, or cilantro)
- Kosher salt and black pepper to taste
- 2 tbsps. unsalted butter
- 4 oz. fresh goat cheese

## Directions

1. Whisk together the eggs, herbs, salt, and pepper.
2. Melt 1 tbsp. butter in a skillet.
3. Put ½ the egg mixture and cook for 4–5 minutes, or until just set.
4. Crumble half the goat cheese over the eggs and fold in half.
5. Cook for 1 minute, or until cheese is melted. Transfer to a plate.
6. Repeat process with the remaining butter, egg mixture, and goat cheese.
7. Serve.

## Nutrition

- Calories: 523

- Fat: 43 g.
- Carb: 3 g.
- Protein: 31 g.

## 5. Bacon and Zucchini Egg Breakfast

**Preparation time:** 10 minutes

**Cooking time:** 10 minutes

**Servings:** 2

## Ingredients

- 2 c. zucchini noodles
- 2 slices of raw bacon
- ¼ c. grated Asiago cheese
- 2 eggs
- Salt and pepper to taste

## Directions

1. Cut the bacon slices into ¼-inch thick strips.
2. Cook the bacon in a pan for 3 minutes.
3. Add the zucchini and mix well.
4. Season with salt and pepper.
5. Flatten slightly with a spatula and make 2 depressions for the eggs.
6. Sprinkle with the cheese.
7. Break one egg into each dent.
8. Cook 3 minutes more, then cover and cook for 2–4 minutes, or until the eggs are cooked.
9. Serve.

## Nutrition

- Calories: 242
- Fat: 19 g.
- Carb: 4 g.
- Protein: 14 g.

# 6. Chia Breakfast Bowl

**Preparation time:** 10 minutes

**Cooking time:** 0 minutes

**Servings:** 2

## Ingredients

- ¼ c. whole chia seeds
- 2 c. almond milk, unsweetened
- 2 tbsps. sugar-free maple syrup
- 1 tsp. vanilla extract

## Toppings:

- Cinnamon and extra maple syrup
- Nuts and berries

## Directions

1. Combine the syrup, milk, chia seeds, and vanilla extract in a bowl and stir to mix.
2. Let stand for 30 minutes, then whisk.
3. Transfer to an airtight container.
4. Cover and refrigerate overnight.
5. Serve in the morning with your desired toppings.

## Nutrition

- Calories: 298
- Fat: 15 g.
- Carb: 5 g.
- Protein: 14 g.

# 7. Cinnamon Roll Oatmeal

**Preparation time:** 10 minutes

**Cooking time:** 10 minutes

**Servings:** 2

## Ingredients

- ⅓ c. crushed pecans
- 1 tbsp. flaxseed meal
- 1 tbsp. chia seeds
- 2 tbsps. cauliflower, riced
- 1 c. plus 1 tbsp. coconut milk
- 1 tbsp. heavy cream
- 1 oz. cream cheese
- 1 tbsp. butter
- ½ tsp. cinnamon
- ½ tsp. maple flavor
- ¼ tsp. vanilla essence
- Pinch of nutmeg
- Pinch of allspice
- 1 tbsp. Erythritol, powdered
- 5 drops liquid Stevia
- Pinch of Xanthan gum

## Directions

1. In a bowl, add flax seeds and chia seeds and set aside.
2. Heat the coconut milk in a saucepan. Once warm, add the cauliflower and cook until it starts to boil.
3. Lower the heat and add allspice, nutmeg, vanilla, maple flavor, and cinnamon.
4. Add Stevia, Erythritol and xanthan gum to the pan and stir well.
5. Add the chia seed and flaxseed mixture to the pan and mix well.
6. Once the mixture is hot, add the cream, cream cheese, butter, and pecans.
7. Mix well and serve.

## Nutrition

- Calories: 398
- Fat: 37.8 g.
- Carb: 3.1 g.
- Protein: 8.8 g.

# 8. Turkey and Scrambled Eggs Breakfast

**Preparation time:** 10 minutes

**Cooking time:** 15 minutes

**Servings:** 2

## Ingredients

- 4 slices avocado
- Salt and pepper to taste
- 4 slices bacon, diced
- 4 turkey breast slices, cooked
- 4 tbsps. coconut oil
- 4 eggs, whisked

## Directions

1. Heat a pan over medium heat.
2. Add bacon slices and brown all over.
3. Heat oil in another pan.
4. Add eggs, salt, and pepper, and scramble.
5. Divide turkey breast slices, bacon, scrambled eggs, and avocado slices on 2 plates and serve.

## Nutrition

- Calories: 791
- Fat: 64.3 g.
- Carb: 8.8 g.
- Protein: 41.8 g.

# 9. Breakfast Cereal

**Preparation time:** 5 minutes

**Cooking time:** 3 minutes

**Servings:** 2

## Ingredients

- ½ c. shredded coconut, unsweetened
- 4 tsps. butter
- 2 c. almond milk, unsweetened
- 1 tbsp. Stevia
- Pinch of salt
- 2 tbsps. macadamia nuts, chopped
- 2 tbsps. walnuts, chopped
- ⅓ c. flaxseed

## Directions

1. Melt the butter in a pan.
2. Add the coconut, milk, salt, nuts, flaxseed, and Stevia, and stir well.
3. Cook for 3 minutes and stir again.
4. Remove from heat. Set aside for 10 minutes.
5. Serve.

## Nutrition

- Calories: 588
- Fat: 48 g.
- Carb: 6.8 g.
- Protein: 16.5 g.

# 10. Best Intermittent Bread

**Preparation time:** 10 minutes

**Cooking time:** 30 minutes

**Servings:** 20

## Ingredients

- 1 ½ c. almond flour
- 6 drops liquid Stevia
- 1 pinch pink Himalayan salt
- ¼ tsp. cream of tartar
- 3 tsps. baking powder
- ¼ c. butter, melted
- 6 large eggs, separated

## Directions

1. Preheat the oven to 375°F.
2. To the egg whites, add cream of tartar and beat until soft peaks are formed.
3. In a food processor, combine Stevia, salt, baking powder, almond flour, melted butter, ⅓ the beaten egg whites, and egg yolks. Mix well.
4. Then add the remaining ⅔ of the egg whites and gently process until fully mixed. Don't over mix.
5. Put grease on an (8x4-inch) loaf pan and pour the mixture into it.
6. Bake for 30 minutes.
7. Enjoy.

## Nutrition

- Calories: 90
- Fat: 7 g.
- Carb: 2 g.
- Protein: 3 g.

## 11. Savory Intermittent Pancake

**Preparation time:** 5 minutes

**Cooking time:** 5 minutes

**Servings:** 2

### Ingredients

- ¼ c. almond flour
- ½ tbsp. unsalted butter
- 2 eggs
- 1 oz. cream cheese, softened

### Directions

1. Bring out a bowl, crack eggs in it, whisk well until fluffy, and then whisk in flour and cream cheese until well combined.
2. Bring out a skillet pan, put it over medium heat, add butter and when it melts, drop pancake batter in four sections, spread it evenly, and cook for 2 minutes per side until brown.

### Nutrition

- Calories: 167
- Fat:15 g.
- Protein: 2 g.
- Carbohydrates: 1 g.

# 12. Bread De Soul

**Preparation time:** 10 minutes

**Cooking time:** 45 minutes

**Servings:** 16

## Ingredients

- ¼ tsp. cream of tartar
- 2 ½ tsp. baking powder
- tsp. Xanthan gum
- ⅓ tsp. baking soda
- ½ tsp. salt
- ⅔ c. unflavored whey protein
- ¼ c. olive oil
- ¼ c. heavy whipping cream
- Drops of sweet leaf Stevia
- eggs
- ¼ c. butter
- 12 oz. softened cream cheese

## Directions

1. Preheat the oven to 325°F.
2. In a bowl, microwave cream cheese and butter for 1 minute.
3. Remove and blend well with a hand mixer.
4. Add olive oil, eggs, heavy cream, and few drops of sweetener and blend well.
5. Put together the dry ingredients in a separate bowl.
6. Combine the dry ingredients with the wet ingredients and mix with a spoon. Don't use a hand blender to avoid whipping it too much.
7. Grease a bread pan and pour the mixture into the pan.
8. Bake in the oven until golden brown for about 45 minutes.
9. Cool and serve.

## Nutrition

- Calories: 200
- Fat: 15.2 g.
- Carb: 1.8 g.
- Protein: 10 g.

# 13. Chia Seed Bread

**Preparation time:** 10 minutes

**Cooking time:** 4 minutes

**Servings:** 16

## Ingredients

- ½ tsp. Xanthan gum
- ½ c. butter
- 2 tbsps. coconut oil
- Tbsp. baking powder
- Tbsp. sesame seeds
- Tbsp. chia seeds
- ½ tsp. salt
- ¼ c. sunflower seeds
- 2 c. almond flour
- 7 eggs

## Directions

1. Preheat the oven to 350°F.
2. Beat eggs in a bowl for 1–2 minutes.
3. Beat in the Xanthan gum and combine coconut oil and melted butter into eggs, beating continuously.
4. Set aside the sesame seeds, but add the rest of the ingredients.
5. Get a loaf pan with baking paper and place the mixture in it. Top the mixture with sesame seeds.
6. Bake in the oven for about 35–40 minutes.

## Nutrition

- Calories: 405
- Fat: 37 g.
- Carb: 4 g.
- Protein: 14 g.

# 14. Special Intermittent Bread

**Preparation time:** 15 minutes

**Cooking time:** 40 minutes

**Servings:** 14

## Ingredients

- 2 tsps. baking powder
- ½ c. water
- tbsp. poppy seeds
- c. fine ground almond meal
- 5 large eggs
- ½ c. olive oil
- ½ tsp. fine Himalayan salt

## Directions

1. Preheat the oven to 400°F.
2. In a bowl, combine salt, almond meal, and baking powder.
3. Drip in oil while mixing, until it forms a crumbly dough.
4. Make a little round hole in the middle of the dough and pour eggs into the middle of the dough.
5. Pour water and whisk eggs together with the mixer in the small circle until it is frothy.
6. Start making larger circles to combine the almond meal mixture with the dough until you have a smooth and thick batter.
7. Line your loaf pan with parchment paper.
8. Pour batter into the loaf pan and sprinkle poppy seeds on top.
9. Bake in the oven for 40 minutes in the center rack until firm and golden brown.
10. Cool in the oven for 30 minutes.
11. Slice and serve.

## Nutrition

- Calories: 22
- Fat: 21 g.
- Carb: 4 g.
- Protein: 7 g.

## 15. Low-Carb Bacon Muffins

**Preparation time:** 15 minutes

**Cooking time:** 25 minutes

**Servings:** 6

### Ingredients

- 2 eggs
- 4 oz. sour cream
- 2 oz. butter
- 4 oz. low-carb flour
- 4 oz. cheese
- 4 oz. bacon
- Salt, to taste

### Directions

1. Whisk the eggs. Combine them with melted butter, sour cream, and flour. Mix well.
2. Cut bacon thinly. Grind the cheese and then combine these two.
3. Join 2 mixtures together and fill muffin molds with the resulting combination.
4. Bake for 25 minutes at 220°F.
5. Enjoy!

### Nutrition

- Calories: 85
- Total fat: 6 g.
- Net carbs: 7 g.
- Protein: 2 g.
- Fiber: 6 g.

## 16. Sausage Quiche

**Preparation time:** 15 minutes

**Cooking time:** 45 minutes

**Servings:** 6

### Ingredients

- 12 oz. pork sausage
- 5 eggplants
- 10 mixed cherry tomatoes, halved
- 6 eggs, beaten
- 2 tsps. whipping cream
- 2 tbsps. Parmesan cheese, grated
- 2 tbsps. fresh parsley, chopped
- Salt and ground black pepper to taste

### Directions

1. Chop sausage and place it on the bottom of a baking dish.
2. Slice eggplants and lay on top.
3. Lay cherry tomatoes on eggplants.
4. In a medium bowl, put and combine eggs, cream, Parmesan cheese, parsley, salt, and pepper. Pour mixture over tomatoes.
5. Preheat the oven to 375°F.
6. Set the baking dish in the oven and cook for 40 minutes.
7. Top with parsley and serve.

### Nutrition

- Calories: 338
- Carbs: 2.9 g.
- Fat: 27.5 g.
- Protein: 17.1 g.

# 17. Cream Cheese Soufflé

**Preparation time:** 15 minutes

**Cooking time:** 20 minutes

**Servings:** 4

## Ingredients

- ⅓ c. spinach, chopped roughly
- 1 tsp. coconut oil
- ¼ c. white onion, peeled and diced
- 1 egg, beaten
- ½ c. cream cheese
- ¼ c. coconut flour
- 1 tsp. salt
- 1 tsp. paprika

## Directions

1. Place spinach in blender or food processor and blend until texture smooth.
2. Preheat the pan with coconut oil on medium heat.
3. Add onion and sauté for about 5 minutes, stirring constantly, until onion turns golden brown.
4. In a medium bowl, combine egg, cream cheese, and coconut flour.
5. Season mixture with salt and paprika, stir well.
6. Add the cooked onion to the mixture and stir.
7. Pour soufflé in baking dish.
8. Place dish in the oven at 365°F. and bake for 10 minutes.
9. Remove the baking dish from the oven and whisk it carefully. Serve.

## Nutrition

- Calories: 196
- Carbs: 5.3 g.
- Fat: 16.9 g.
- Protein: 5.6 g.

## 18. 3-Cheese Pizza Frittata

**Preparation time:** 10 minutes

**Cooking time:** 40 minutes

**Servings:** 4

### Ingredients

- ¼ c. Ricotta cheese
- 1 oz. pepperoni, sliced
- 2 ½ oz. Mozzarella cheese, shredded
- 6 eggs (large ones)
- ¼ c. Parmesan cheese, grated
- 5 oz. frozen spinach, thawed
- ½ tsp. Italian seasoning, dried
- 2 tbsps. olive oil
- Salt and pepper, to taste
- Nonstick cooking spray

### Directions

1. Preheat the oven to 375°F.
2. Use a cooking spray to grease the pie plate and keep it aside.
3. Place the frozen spinach in the microwave and defrost for 5 minutes. Once done, squeeze out the water completely.
4. Get a large bowl and break the eggs into it.
5. Add the salt, pepper, olive oil, and Italian seasoning into the cracked eggs in the bowl.
6. Whisk the contents together until well combined.
7. Now, add the drained spinach, Parmesan cheese, and Ricotta cheese into the egg mixture.
8. Mix the contents thoroughly until they are incorporated well.
9. Put this mixture into the greased pie plate and top it with pepperoni and Mozzarella
10. Bake for 40 minutes until the cheese is slightly browned and the egg is perfectly set.
11. Take off from the oven and allow it cool for some time.
12. Slice the pies and transfer them to a plate. Serve hot and enjoy!

### Nutrition

- Calories: 301.13
- Fat: 13.48 g.

- Protein: 18.87 g.
- Net carb: 2.74 g.

## 19. **Baked Omelet With Bacon**

**Preparation time:** 5 minutes

**Cooking time:** 30 minutes

**Servings:** 1

### Ingredients

- 4 eggs
- 140 g. diced bacon
- 85 g. butter
- 60 g. fresh spinach
- l finely chopped fresh onions
- Salt and pepper

### Directions

1. Preheat the oven to 400°F. Oil one small baking dish (per serving).
2. Fry the bacon and spinach in the remaining oil.
3. In another bowl, whisk the eggs until it's foamy. Mix the bacon and spinach, gradually adding the fat remaining after frying the products.
4. Then add finely chopped onions. Flavor the dish with salt and pepper.
5. Put the mixture into a baking sheet then bake for at least 20 minutes or until golden brown.
6. Recover the dish and let it cool for a few minutes. After that, you can serve.

### Nutrition

- Carbohydrates: 12 g.
- Fat: 72 g.
- Protein: 21 g.
- Calories: 737 g.

## 20. Easy Cloud Buns

**Preparation time:** 10 minutes

**Cooking time:** 30 minutes

**Servings:** 10

### Ingredients

- 3 oz. chopped cream cheese
- 8 tsps. cream of tartar
- 3 eggs, separated (large ones)

### Directions

1. Preheat the oven to 300°F.
2. Line a baking tray using parchment and set it aside.
3. Place the egg whites in a large bowl and beat them until foamy.
4. Add in the cream of tartar to the beaten egg whites and whisk well until you see soft peaks and the whites look shiny.
5. Take another medium-sized bowl and place the egg yolks in it.
6. Add the cream cheese to the egg yolks and beat them together until combined well.
7. Put the egg white mixture into the yolk mixture carefully.
8. Spoon this batter in ¼ c. circle format on the lined baking sheet.
9. Leave 2-inch gap between each circle and bake for 30 minutes until firm.
10. Remove from the oven and let it cool.
11. Transfer to a plate and serve warm. Enjoy!

### Nutrition

- Calories: 76
- Fat: 6 g.
- Protein: 3 g.
- Net carb: 0 g.

# 21. Coconut Pancakes

**Preparation time:** 10 minutes

**Cooking time:** 10 minutes

**Servings:** 2

## Ingredients

- 4 tbsps. coconut flour
- 3 oz. coconut milk
- 2 eggs
- 1 tbsp. melted coconut oil
- Pinch salt
- ½ tsp. baking powder
- 1 oz. coconut oil (or butter) for frying
- 1 tsp. Erythritol (optional)

## Directions

1. If you want fluffy pancakes, separate the egg whites and whisk them with a pinch of salt until stiff peaks form. If you don't have enough time, skip this step.
2. In another bowl, mix the egg yolks (wholes egg if you skip the first step), coconut milk, and melted coconut oil (it has to be at room temperature so it doesn't burn egg yolks).
3. Add in coconut flour, baking powder, and sweetener (if using) and mix well until smooth.
4. Slowly transfer the egg whites to the batter. Set aside for 3–5 minutes.
5. Preheat an oiled (or buttered) skillet at medium-low heat. Fry pancakes for 2–4 minutes on both sides until golden brown. Flip them gently.
6. Serve coconut pancakes with sour cream, whipped cream, or your favorite intermittent-friendly toppings (do not forget about carbs in berries and cream).

## Nutrition

- Calories: 328
- Total carbs: 9 g.
- Fiber: 5 g.
- Net carbs: 4 g.
- Fat: 28 g.
- Protein: 9 g.

## 22. Almond Pancakes

**Preparation time:** 5 minutes

**Cooking time:** 15 minutes

**Servings:** 2

## Ingredients

- ½ c. almond flour
- 1 egg
- 2½ tbsps. unsweetened almond milk
- 2 tbsps. coconut oil, divided (1 tbsp. for batter, 1 tbsp. for frying)
- 1 tbsp. Erythritol (optional; use if you want a sweet taste)
- Pinch salt (if using sweetener)
- ½ tsp. baking powder
- ½ tsp. pure vanilla extract (optional)

## Directions

1. In a bowl, put and mix all the ingredients except 1 tbsp. coconut oil with a whisk until smooth.
2. Place an oiled pan over medium-low heat. Pour heaping tbsps. batter onto the pan and form pancakes. Cover and fry for about 1–2 minutes, then flip pancakes when bubbles start to form and cook for another 1–2 minutes.
3. Transfer pancakes to the plate and repeat the cooking process until the batter is used up.
4. Serve whipped cream or sour cream and berries (do not forget about carbs in berries and cream).

## Nutrition

- Calories: 325
- Total carbs: 7 g.
- Fiber: 4 g.
- Net carbs: 3 g.
- Fat: 30 g.
- Protein: 9 g.

## 23. Cottage Cheese Pancakes

**Preparation time:** 5 minutes

**Cooking time:** 15 minutes

**Servings:** 2

### Ingredients

- ½ lb. cheese
- 2 eggs
- ½ tbsp. psyllium husk powder
- 4 oz. heavy whipping cream
- 1 oz. coconut oil (or butter) for frying

### Directions

1. Mix cottage cheese, eggs, and psyllium husk powder in a bowl, until well combined. Set the mixture aside for 5–7 minutes to thicken.
2. Place an oiled pan over medium-low heat. Pour 2-inch circles of batter onto the pan and try to make small-sized pancakes. It's easier to flip smaller pancakes. Fry pancakes for 2–4 minutes on both sides until golden brown.
3. In another bowl, whip heavy cream to soft peaks.
4. Serve the cottage cheese pancakes with whipped cream and enjoy!

### Nutrition

- Calories: 473
- Total carbs: 7 g.
- Fiber: 2 g.
- Net carbs: 5 g.
- Fat: 43 g.
- Protein: 16 g.

## 24. Eggs and Bell Peppers

**Preparation time:** 5 minutes

**Cooking time:** 20 minutes

**Servings:** 4

### Ingredients

- Red bell pepper, cut into strips
- 1 green bell pepper, cut into strips
- 1 orange bell pepper, cut into strips
- 4 eggs, whisked
- Salt and black pepper to the taste
- 2 tbsps. Mozzarella, shredded
- Cooking spray

### Directions

1. In a bowl, mix the eggs with all the bell peppers, salt, and pepper and toss.
2. Heat up the air fryer at 350°F, grease it with cooking spray, pour the eggs mixture, spread well, sprinkle the Mozzarella on top, and cook for 20 minutes.
3. Divide between plates and serve for breakfast.

### Nutrition

- Calories: 229
- Fat: 13 g.
- Fiber: 3 g.
- Carbohydrates: 4 g.
- Protein: 7 g.

## 25. Herbed Eggs Mix

**Preparation time:** 5 minutes

**Cooking time:** 20 minutes

**Servings:** 4

### Ingredients

- 10 eggs, whisked
- ½ c. cheddar, shredded
- 2 tbsps. parsley, chopped
- 2 tbsps. chives, chopped
- 2 tbsps. basil, chopped
- Cooking spray
- Salt and black pepper to the taste

### Directions

1. In a bowl, mix the eggs with all the ingredients except the cheese and the cooking spray and whisk well.
2. Heat the air fryer at 350°F, grease it with the cooking spray, and pour the eggs mixture inside.
3. Scatter the cheese on top and cook for 20 minutes.
4. Divide everything between plates and serve.

### Nutrition

- Calories: 232
- Fat: 12 g.
- Fiber: 4 g.
- Carbohydrates: 5 g.
- Protein: 7 g.

## 26. Cherry Tomatoes Omelet

**Preparation time:** 5 minutes

**Cooking time:** 20 minutes

**Servings:** 4

### Ingredients

- 4 eggs, whisked
- 1 lb. cherry tomatoes, halved
- 1 tbsp. parsley, chopped
- Cooking spray
- 1 tbsp. cheddar, grated
- Salt and black pepper to the taste

### Directions

1. Put the tomatoes in the air fryer's basket, cook at 360°F. for 5 minutes and transfer them to the baking pan that fits the machine greased with cooking spray.
2. In a bowl, mix the eggs with the remaining ingredients, whisk, pour over the tomatoes, and heat at 360°F for 15 minutes.
3. Serve right away for breakfast.

### Nutrition

- Calories: 230
- Fat: 14
- Fiber: 3 g.
- Carbohydrates: 5 g.
- Protein: 11 g.

# 27. Zucchini Spread

**Preparation time:** 5 minutes

**Cooking time:** 15 minutes

**Servings:** 4

## Ingredients

- 4 zucchinis, roughly chopped
- 1 tbsp. sweet paprika
- Salt and black pepper to the taste
- 1 tbsp. butter, melted

## Directions

1. Grease a baking pan that fits the air fryer with the butter, add all the ingredients, toss, and cook at 360°F for 15 minutes.
2. Transfer to a blender, pulse well, divide into bowls and serve for breakfast.

## Nutrition

- Calories: 240
- Fat: 14 g.
- Fiber: 2 g.
- Carbohydrates: 5 g.
- Protein: 11 g.

## 28. Intermittent Cheese Tacos

**Preparation time:** 15 minutes

**Cooking time:** 20 minutes

**Servings:** 6

### Ingredients

- 3 strips of bacon
- 1 oz. cheddar cheese, shredded
- ½ avocado
- 1 tbsp. butter
- 1 c. Mozzarella cheese, shredded
- 6 large eggs
- Salt and pepper, to taste

### Directions

1. Start by thoroughly cooking the bacon. Either in the oven for at least 15–20 minutes at 375°F or on the stovetop.
2. Heat a pan in medium heat and add ⅓ c. Mozzarella.
3. Cook the cheese until it begins to bubble and turn brown on the side touching the pan. Pay close attention here!
4. Slip a spatula under the cheese and carefully unstick it from the pan.
5. Using a pair of tongs, drape the cheese over a wooden spoon, that should be resting over a bowl or pot. Let the cheese cool and form a taco shell shape.
6. Repeat Steps 2–5 with the remaining Mozzarella.
7. Add the butter and eggs to the pan and cook thoroughly, adding salt and pepper to suit your taste.
8. Divide the eggs equally between your cheese shells.
9. Slice the avocado and divide the slices evenly between the tacos.
10. Chop or crumble your bacon, and divide equally between the tacos.
11. Sprinkle your cheddar cheese over the tops.

### Nutrition

- Calories: 30
- Total fat: 2.5 g.
- Net carbs: 0.5 g.
- Protein: 1.5 g.

- Fiber: 11.6 g.

# 29. Intermittent Mini Doughnuts

**Preparation time:** 15 minutes

**Cooking time:** 10 minutes

**Servings:** 22

## Ingredients

- 4 tbsps. almond flour
- tbsp. coconut flour
- 1 tsp. vanilla extract
- 1 tsp. baking powder
- 4 tbsps. Erythritol
- 2 oz. cream cheese
- 3 large eggs
- 10 drops liquid Stevia

## Directions

1. Combine with an immersion blender or a food processor.
2. Make sure that all your ingredients are well blended and smooth.
3. Heat your doughnut maker and spray with your grease of choice. Coconut oil always gives your cooking a delicious finish! Pour your mixture into the doughnut maker. Leave some room (say 10%) to give your doughnuts space to rise.
4. Let the mixture cook for 3 minutes, and then flip and cook for an additional 2 minutes.
5. Remove the baked doughnuts and repeat steps 3–5 for the rest of your batter.

## Nutrition

- Calories: 30
- Total fat: 2.5 g.
- Net carbs: 0.5 g.
- Protein: 1.5 g.
- Fiber: 11.6 g.

## 30. Delicious Flax Pancakes

**Preparation time:** 5 minutes

**Cooking time:** 20 minutes

**Servings:** 3

### Ingredients

- 150 g. fat sour cream
- 4 eggs
- ½ tsp. salt
- 1 tsp. baking powder
- 50 g. room temperature butter
- 6 tsp. with a hill of ground flax seeds
- Sweetener to taste
- 20 g. any fat for frying

### Directions

1. Using a mixer, beat the butter, add the eggs, sour cream, baking powder, salt, and sweetener and beat until smooth all together
2. Add one spoonful of flax and continue to whisk.
3. The dough should turn out as it is for pancakes, that is, as a thick sour cream.
4. Heat the pan, put the oil in, and fry as usual. But layout the circles thickly and with a diameter of about 4 cm., because they sprawl out and become larger.
5. Fry over low heat, otherwise they will burn.

### Nutrition

- Carbohydrates: 1.42 g.
- Fat: 7.20 g.
- Protein: 2.08 g.
- Calories: 75.69

## 31. Intermittent Fluffy Cloud Bread

**Preparation time:** 25 minutes

**Cooking time:** 25 minutes

**Servings:** 3

### Ingredients

- Pinch salt
- ½ tbsp. ground psyllium husk powder
- ½ tbsp. baking powder
- ¼ tsp. cream of tartar
- 3 eggs, separated
- ½ c., cream cheese

### Directions

1. Preheat the oven to 300°F.
2. Whisk egg whites in a bowl until soft peaks are formed.
3. Mix egg yolks with cream cheese, salt, cream of tartar, psyllium husk powder, and baking powder in a bowl.
4. Fold in the egg whites carefully and transfer to the baking tray.
5. Place in the oven and bake for 25 minutes.
6. Remove from the oven and serve.

### Nutrition

- Calories: 185
- Fat: 16.4 g.
- Carb: 3.9 g.
- Protein: 6.6 g.

## 32. Parmesan Cheese and Baby Spinach Omelet

**Preparation time:** 6 minutes

**Cooking time:** 9 minutes

**Servings:** 1

### Ingredients

- 1½ tbsps. Parmesan cheese, grated
- 1 c. baby spinach leaves, torn
- 1 egg
- ⅛ tsp. ground nutmeg
- ¼ tsp. onion powder
- Salt and ground black pepper, to taste
- 1 tbsp. olive oil

### Directions

1. Whisk the eggs in a large bowl, then mix in the grated Parmesan cheese and spinach. Sprinkle the nutmeg, onion powder, salt, and ground black pepper to season.
2. To make the omelet, drizzle a nonstick skillet with olive oil and heat over medium heat. Pour in the mixture and cook for 6 minutes, flipping the omelet halfway through the cooking time.
3. Lower the heat and cook for 2–3 minutes more until the omelet reaches your desired doneness.
4. Top the cooked omelet with ketchup, if desired, and slice to serve.

### Nutrition

- Calories: 301
- Total fat: 21.6 g.
- Carbs: 4.8 g.
- Protein: 21 g.
- Cholesterol: 1244 mg.
- Sodium: 367 mg.

# 33. Ritzy Mushroom and Olive Omelet

**Preparation time:** 15 minutes

**Cooking time:** 30 minutes

**Servings:** 8

## Ingredients

- 1 (12 oz./340 g.) can of mushrooms, sliced
- 1 (6 oz./170 g.) can of black olives, sliced
- 12 eggs, scrambled
- ¼ c. butter
- 1 small onion, chopped
- ½ c. coconut milk
- ½ tsp. salt
- ½ tsp. ground black pepper
- 1 ½ c. Cheddar cheese, shredded
- Cooked ham, chopped (optional)
- Jalapeño peppers, sliced (optional)

## Directions

1. Start by preheating the oven to 400°F (205°C).
2. Put the butter in a nonstick skillet, and melt over medium heat. Swirl the skillet so the butter covers the bottom evenly. Add the chopped onion and sauté for 5–7 minutes or until translucent. Let it stand for later use.
3. Combine the scrambled eggs with coconut milk in a large bowl, then sprinkle with salt and ground black pepper. Stir to mix well. Set aside.
4. Make the omelet: Put the shredded Cheddar cheese in a greased baking pan, then top the cheese with sautéed onion, ham, mushrooms, olives, and jalapeño, and then pour over the egg mixture.
5. Arrange the baking pan into the preheated oven without stirring the mixture. Bake for 30 minutes, flipping the omelet halfway through the cooking time. To check the doneness, cut a small slit in the center of the omelet.
6. Remove the baked omelet from the oven. Wait for a few minutes and slice to serve.

## Nutrition

- Calories: 344
- Total fat: 27.3 g.

- Carbs: 7.2 g.
- Protein: 17.9 g.
- Cholesterol: 254 mg.
- Sodium: 1087 mg.

## 34. Sausage and Veggies Frittata

**Preparation time:** 10 minutes

**Cooking time:** 30 minutes

**Servings:** 6

### Ingredients

- 8 eggs
- 8 drops hot pepper sauce or more to taste
- 2 tbsps. heavy cream
- 4 oz. (113 g.) bulk breakfast sausage, crumbled
- 2 tbsps. butter
- ⅔ c. red bell pepper, chopped
- ½ c. onion, chopped
- 1 c. mushrooms, chopped
- Salt and ground black pepper, to taste
- ½ c. chopped fresh spinach, blanched
- 1 c. Cheddar cheese, shredded

### Directions

1. Preheat the oven to 325°F (160°C).
2. Whisk together the eggs, hot pepper sauce, and heavy cream. Set aside.
3. To make the frittata, sauté the sausage in a nonstick skillet over medium heat for 4 minutes, then add and melt the butter. Swirl the skillet so the butter coat the bottom evenly.
4. Put the red bell pepper, onion, mushrooms, salt, and ground black pepper and sauté for 4 minutes until the onion is translucent.
5. Add the spinach and sauté for 1 minute. Take out the mixture from the skillet to a baking pan. Sprinkle the cheese on top and pour over the egg mixture.
6. Arrange the pan into the preheated oven and bake for 20 minutes.

170

7. Remove the baking pan from the oven. Wait to cool for a few minutes, and slice to serve.

## Nutrition

- Calories: 283
- Total fat: 22.7 g.
- Carbs: 3.8 g.
- Protein: 16.5 g.
- Cholesterol: 295 mg.
- Sodium: 443 mg.

# 35. Sausage Breakfast Casserole

**Preparation time:** 15 minutes

**Cooking time:** 21 minutes

**Servings:** 4

## Ingredients

- lbs. (680 g.) pork sausage, crumbled
- 1 (8 oz./227 g.) package of gluten-free crescent roll
- 4 eggs, beaten
- C. Mozzarella cheese, shredded
- ¾ c. coconut milk
- Salt and ground black pepper, to taste

## Directions

1. Preheat the oven to 425°F (220°C).
2. Heat the sausage in a nonstick skillet over medium heat for 6 minutes until browned. Transfer the cooked sausage into a large bowl.
3. Add the beaten eggs, Mozzarella cheese, coconut milk, salt, and ground black pepper to the bowl. Stir to combine well. Set aside.
4. Flatten the crescent rolls on a clean working surface with a rolling pin. Lay the flattened crescent rolls on a greased casserole dish.
5. Pour the sausage mixture over the crescent rolls. Arrange the casserole dish into the preheated oven and bake for 15 minutes.

171

6. Take out the casserole dish from the oven and allow it to cool before serving.

## Nutrition

- Calories: 389
- Total fat: 31.8 g.
- Carbs: 9.3 g.
- Protein: 15.1 g.
- Cholesterol: 114 mg.
- Sodium: 671 mg.

## 36. Scrambled Egg and Sausage Muffins

**Preparation time:** 10 minutes

**Cooking time:** 20 minutes

**Servings:** 4

### Ingredients

- 12 eggs
- 8 oz. (227 g.) bulk pork sausage, crumbled
- 2 tbsps. olive oil
- ½ c. onion, chopped
- ½ c. chopped green bell pepper, or to taste
- ½ c. Cheddar cheese, shredded
- ¼ tsp. garlic powder
- ½ tsp. salt
- ¼ tsp. ground black pepper

### Directions

1. Start by preheating the oven to 350ºF (180ºC).
2. Warm a nonstick skillet over medium heat. Put the sausage and sauté for 10 minutes or until well browned. Remove from the skillet and set aside.
3. Clean the skillet and drizzle with olive oil. Add the chopped onion into the skillet and sauté for 3 minutes or until the onion is half translucent, then break the eggs into the skillet and sauté for 3 minutes or until the eggs are scrambled, and then add the green bell pepper, shredded cheese, garlic powder, salt, and ground black pepper and cook for 2 minutes more until the cheese melts.
4. Fold in the cooked sausage and sauté to combine. Spoon ⅓ c. the mixture in a muffin cup. Repeat with the remaining mixture and muffin cup. Arrange the muffin cup. in the preheated oven.
5. Bake for 20 minutes or until the tops of the muffins spring back when gently pressed with your fingers.
6. Remove from the oven. Allow it to cool for a few minutes before serving.

### Nutrition

- Calories: 196
- Total fat: 14.9 g.
- Carbs: 2.1 g.

- Protein: 12.7 g.
- Cholesterol: 202 mg.
- Sodium: 365 mg.

## 37. Eggs in Avocado Boat

**Preparation time:** 10 minutes

**Cooking time:** 25 minutes

**Servings:** 2

### Ingredients

- 1 tsp. coconut oil
- 1 large ripe avocado (cut in half, pit removed and enough flesh scooped out to hold an egg)
- 2 eggs
- Salt and pepper to taste
- Fresh thyme to garnish

### Directions

1. Remove a portion of the skin on the back of the avocado so it can sit straight.
2. Crack the eggs and place them in separate containers. Place the whites together in a bowl and place the yolks in individual shot glasses. salt and pepper to taste and mix well.
3. Heat coconut oil in a skillet.
4. Add the avocado halves (flesh side down) and sear until slightly golden, about 30 seconds.
5. Flip the avocados and fill the middle with egg whites.
6. Lower the heat, cover with a lid, and cook until the egg whites are almost set about 15–20 minutes. Slide the yolks over the whites.
7. Continue to cook until yolks have cooked, about 3–5 minutes.
8. Place on a plate and garnish with thyme.
9. Serve.

### Nutrition

- Calories: 215
- Fat: 18.1 g.
- Carb: 6 g.
- Protein: 9.1 g.

# 38. Splendid Low-Carb Bread

**Preparation time:** 15 minutes

**Cooking time:** 60–70 minutes

**Servings:** 12

## Ingredients

- ½ tsp. herbs, such as basil, rosemary, or oregano
- ½ tsp. garlic or onion powder
- ½ tbsp. baking powder
- 5 tbsps. psyllium husk powder
- ½ c. almond flour
- ½ c. coconut flour
- ¼ tsp. salt
- ½ c. egg whites
- 1 tbsp. oil or melted butter
- ½ tbsp. apple cider vinegar
- ⅓–¾ c. hot water

## Directions

1. Put grease on a loaf pan and preheat the oven to 350°F.
2. In a bowl, whisk the salt, psyllium husk powder, onion or garlic powder, coconut flour, almond flour, and baking powder.
3. Stir in egg whites, oil, and apple cider vinegar. Bit by bit add the hot water, stirring until dough increase in size. Do not add too much water.
4. Mold the dough into a rectangle and transfer to a grease loaf pan.
5. Bake in the oven for 60–70 minutes, or until the crust feels firm and brown on top.
6. Cool and serve.

## Nutrition

- Calories: 97
- Fat: 5.7 g.
- Carb: 7.5 g.
- Protein: 4.1 g.

# 39. Pumpkin Pancakes

**Preparation time:** 5 minutes

**Cooking time:** 12–15 minutes

**Servings:** 2

## Ingredients

- 1 egg
- 1 egg white
- 1 tbsp. cream cheese
- 1½ tbsp. canned pumpkin, unsweetened
- ½ tbsp. vanilla extract
- ⅓ c. almond flour
- 1 tbsp. coconut flour
- ½ tbsp. Swerve sweetener
- ½ tsp. pumpkin pie spice
- Pinch of salt
- ½ tsp. baking powder
- Pinch of baking soda
- ¼ tsp. Xanthan gum
- Water as needed

## Directions

1. Preheat a griddle to 350°F. Add all the wet pancake ingredients except the water to a blender and blend. Now add the dry ingredients.
2. Continue to blend until smooth.
3. Add water until pancake batter has the right consistency.
4. Into the preheated, oiled griddle, pour a small amount of batter.
5. Cook until browned and the edges almost to the center are dry about 3–4 minutes.
6. Then flip and heat for 2–3 minutes.
7. Repeat to finish the batter and serve.

## Nutrition

- Calories: 230
- Fat: 16 g.
- Carb: 9.5 g.
- Protein: 8 g.

# 40. Buttermilk Pancakes

**Preparation time:** 5 minutes

**Cooking time:** 8 minutes

**Servings:** 2

## Ingredients

- 1 ½ tbsp. coconut flour
- 1 ½ tbsp. almond flour
- 1 egg
- 2 tbsps. almond milk + ¼ tsp. apple cider vinegar, mixed in a bowl
- ¼ tsp. vanilla extract
- Pinch of baking powder
- ½ tsp. Erythritol
- 1 tsp. butter, melted
- Pinch of sea salt

## Directions

1. Mix all the ingredients in a bowl.
2. Heat a lightly greased skillet over medium-high heat. Make sure the skillet is hot.
3. Spoon batter onto the skillet and cook until the batter starts to bubble about 2 minutes. Then flip and cook until the middle is done. Adjust the heat if needed.
4. Repeat with the remaining batter.
5. Serve with condiments of choice.

## Nutrition

- Calories: 81
- Fat: 6 g.
- Carb: 4 g.
- Protein: 3 g.

# Lunch

## 41. Cauliflower Pizza

**Preparation time:** 10 minutes

**Cooking time:** 20 minutes

**Servings:** 2

## Ingredients

- 1 c. cauliflower
- ½ c. grated Mozzarella
- 1 organic egg
- 1 c. white ham
- 1 c. Mozzarella
- 4 tbsps. tomato sauce
- ½ c. grated cheese
- 1 tsp. oregano
- 1 cup olives
- 1 cup capers

## Directions

1. Cut the cauliflower head into small florets.
2. Grate the cauliflower; heat it for 4 minutes in the microwave.
3. Fluff the cauliflower with a fork.
4. Mix the egg and grated cheese with drained cauliflower until you obtain the dough.
5. Spread the obtained mixture on a sheet of parchment paper and bake at 400°F until golden brown for about 15–20 minutes.
6. Garnish your pizza with olive and capers.
7. Cut the pizza; then divide the portions between 2 containers and store it in the refrigerator for 2 days.

## Nutrition

- Calories: 430
- Fat: 35.4 g.
- Carbs: 7 g.
- Protein: 22.8 g.

## 42. Chicken Pizzaiola

**Preparation time:** 10 minutes

**Cooking time:** 20 minutes

**Servings:** 3

### Ingredients

- 3 chicken breasts
- 1 tray with ham
- 1 c. pasta sauce
- 1 and ½ c. grated cheese
- 1 pinch of salt and pepper
- 2 tbsps. olive oil

### Directions

1. Preheat the oven to 290°F.
2. Place the 3 chicken breasts on a sheet of parchment paper directly on the plate of the oven.
3. Slice the breasts partially and garnish with sauce, ham, and cheese.
4. Cover with grated cheese, season with salt and pepper, and drizzle with oil.
5. Bake in a hot oven for 20 minutes.
6. Once ready, divide the 2 chicken breasts between three containers.
7. Seal the containers very well and store them in the refrigerator for 3 days.

### Nutrition

- Calories: 453

- Fat: 34.8 g.
- Carbs: 8.9 g.
- Protein: 26 g.
- Sugar: 1.5 g.

## 43. Beef Stroganoff With Protein: Noodles

**Preparation time:** 14 minutes

**Cooking time:** 29 min

**Servings:** 1

### Ingredients

- 2 oz. barilla protein farfalle Pasta
- ½ c. fresh sliced mushrooms
- 2 tbsps. chopped onion
- 1 tbsp. butter
- Dash of black pepper
- 6 oz. steak, sliced thinly
- 1 tbsp. tomato paste
- ¼ tsp. of Dijon mustard
- ½ c. beef broth
- 1 tsp. low-carb flax meal
- ½ small container plain Greek yogurt

## Directions

1. Cook the pasta in water.
2. Place the butter in a Teflon skillet.
3. Next, add in the onions, and mushrooms, cook until the onions are shiny and the water is gone.
4. Add the beef and brown well.
5. Stir in the remaining ingredients except for the pasta and yogurt.
6. Cook this until the beef is done, approximately 9 minutes.
7. Drain the pasta.
8. If the sauce is too thin, add 1 tsp. low-carb flax meal and boil to thicken.
9. Turn back down to low. Then add the yogurt to the sauce.
10. Serve the stroganoff over the pasta.

## Nutrition

- Calories: 559
- Total fat: 23 g.
- Protein: 55 g.
- Total carbs: 4 g.
- Dietary fiber: 13 g.
- Sugar: 2 g.
- Sodium: 957 mg.

## 44. Beefy Tostadas

**Preparation time:** 4 minutes

**Cooking time:** 9 minutes

**Servings:** 2

## Ingredients

- ¼ lb. ground sirloin
- ¼ c. onions, minced
- 1 tsp. garlic, minced
- 1 tbsp. olive oil
- ½ c. chopped green, red, and yellow peppers
- ½ c. cheddar cheese, mild or sharp, hand-shredded
- 2 tortilla factory low-carb tortillas
- 2 tbsps. butter
- 1 c. Greek yogurt, plain
- 2 tbsps. Salsa Verde

## Directions

1. Brown the tortillas in the butter. Place on a warm plate.
2. Cook the sirloin, onions, garlic, peppers in olive oil.
3. Place on the tortillas.
4. Top with the cheese.
5. Add the Greek yogurt.
6. Drizzle with the salsa.

## Nutrition

- Calories: 735
- Total fat: 48 g.
- Protein: 66 g.
- Total carbs: 18 g.
- Dietary fiber: 8 g.
- Sugar: 0 g.
- Sodium: 708 mg.

## 45. Intermittent Chicken Garam Masala

**Preparation time:** 10 minutes

**Cooking time:** 20 minutes

**Servings:** 4

### Ingredients

- 25 oz. chicken breasts
- 3 tbsps. butter or ghee
- Salt
- 1 red bell pepper, finely diced
- 1 ¼ c. coconut cream or heavy whipping cream
- 1 tbsp. fresh parsley, finely chopped

### For the garam masala:

- 1 tsp. ground cumin
- 1–2 tsps. coriander seed, ground
- 1 tsp. ground cardamom (green)
- 1 tsp. turmeric, ground
- 1 tsp. ground ginger
- 1 tsp. paprika powder
- 1 tsp. chili powder
- 1 pinch ground nutmeg

### Directions

1. Preheat the oven to 400°F.
2. Mix the spices together for the garam masala.
3. Cut the chicken breasts lengthwise. Place a large skillet over medium-high heat and fry the chicken in the butter until it is golden brown.
4. Add ½ the Garam masala spice mix to the pan and stir it thoroughly.
5. Season with some salt, and place the chicken and all of the juices, into a baking dish.
6. Finely chop the bell pepper and add it to a bowl along with the coconut cream and the remaining ½ the Garam masala spice mix.
7. Pour over the chicken. Bake for 20 minutes.
8. Garnish with parsley and serve.

## Nutrition

- Calories: 312
- Protein: 21 g.
- Fat: 14 g.
- Net carbs: 2 g

# 46. Intermittent Lasagna

**Preparation time:** 25 minutes

**Cooking time:** 1 hour minutes

**Servings:** 4

## Ingredients

- 2 tbsps. olive oil
- 1 yellow onion
- 1 garlic clove
- 20 oz. ground beef
- 3 tbsps. tomato paste
- ½ tbsp. dried basil
- 1 tsp. salt
- ¼ tsp. ground black pepper
- ½ c. water
- Intermittent pasta
- 8 eggs
- 10 oz. cream cheese
- 1 tsp. salt
- 5 tbsps. ground psyllium husk powder

## For the cheese topping:

- 2 c. crème fraiche or sour cream
- 5 oz. shredded cheese
- 2 oz. grated Parmesan cheese
- ½ tsp. salt

- ¼ tsp. ground black pepper
- ½ c. fresh parsley, finely chopped

## Directions

1. Start with the ground beef mixture.
2. Peel and finely chop the onion and the garlic. Fry them in olive oil until they are soft. Add the ground beef to the onion and garlic and cook until it is golden. Add the tomato paste and the remaining spices.
3. Stir the mixture thoroughly and add some water. Bring it to a boil, turn the heat down, and let it simmer for at least 15 minutes, or until the majority of the water has evaporated. The lasagna sheets used don't soak up as much liquid as regular ones, so the mixture should be quite dry.
4. While that is happening, make the lasagna sheets according to the instructions that follow below.
5. Preheat the oven to 400°F. Mix the shredded cheese with sour cream and the Parmesan cheese. Reserve 1or 2 tbsps. the cheese aside for the topping. Add salt and pepper for tasting and stir in the parsley.
6. Place the lasagna sheets and pasta sauce in layers in a greased baking dish.
7. Spread the crème Fraiche mixture and the reserved Parmesan cheese on top.
8. Bake the lasagna in the oven for around 30 minutes or until the lasagna has a nicely browned surface. Serve with a green salad and a light dressing.

## To make the lasagna sheets:

1. Preheat the oven to 300°F.
2. Add the eggs, cream cheese, and salt to a mixing bowl and blend into a smooth batter. Continue to whisk this while adding in the ground psyllium husk powder, just a little bit at a time. Let it sit for a few minutes.
3. Using a spatula spread the batter onto a baking sheet that is lined with parchment paper. Place more parchment paper on top and flatten it with a rolling pin until the mixture is at least 13" x 18". You can also divide it into two separate batches and use a different baking sheet for even thinner pasta.
4. Let the pieces of parchment paper stay in place. Bake the pasta for about 10–12 minutes. Let it cool and remove the paper. Slice into sheets.

## Nutrition

- Calories: 128
- Protein: 25 g.
- Fat: 15 g.
- Net carbs: 4 g.

## 47. Delicious Creamy Crab Meat

**Preparation time:** 5 minutes

**Cooking time:** 10 minutes

**Servings:** 3

### Ingredients

- 1 lb. crab meat
- ½ c. cream cheese
- 2 tbsps. mayonnaise
- Salt and pepper, to taste
- 1 tbsp. lemon juice
- 1 c. Cheddar cheese, shredded

### Directions

1. Mix cream cheese mayo, pepper, lemon juice, and salt in a bowl. Place in crab meat and make small balls. Place the balls inside the pot. Seal the lid and select Manual.
2. Cook for about 10 minutes on high pressure. When finished, allow the pressure to release naturally for 10 minutes. Sprinkle the cheese.
3. Serve!

### Nutrition

- Calories: 443
- Net carbs: 2.5 g.
- Fat: 30.4 g.
- Protein: 41 g.

## 48. Creamy Broccoli Stew

**Preparation time:** 10 minutes

**Cooking time:** 20 minutes

**Servings:** 4

### Ingredients

- 1 c. heavy cream
- 1 c. broccoli florets
- 3 oz. Parmesan cheese
- 2 carrots, sliced
- ½ tbsp. garlic paste
- ¼ tbsp turmeric powder
- Salt and black pepper, to taste
- 2 tbsps. butter
- ½ c. vegetable broth

### Directions

1. Melt butter on Sauté mode. Put the garlic and sauté for 30 seconds. Add carrots and broccoli and cook until soft, for 2–3 minutes. Season with pepper and salt.
2. Stir in the vegetable broth and seal the lid. Heat on Meat/Stew mode for 40 minutes. When prepared, do a quick pressure release. Stir in the heavy creams.

### Nutrition

- Calories: 239
- Net carbs: 5.1 g.
- Fat: 21.4 g.
- Protein: 8 g.

## 49. No-Crust Tomato and Spinach Quiche

**Preparation time:** 10 minutes

**Cooking time:** 30 minutes

**Servings:** 3

## Ingredients

- 14 large eggs
- Salt to taste
- 1 c. full milk
- 4 c. fresh Baby spinach, chopped
- Ground black pepper to taste
- 2 tomatoes, diced
- 3 scallions, sliced
- 1 tomato, sliced into firm rings
- ½ c. Parmesan cheese, shredded
- Water for boiling

## Directions

1. Place the stand in the pot and dispense in 1½ c. water. Break the eggs into a bowl, add pepper, salt, and milk and whisk it. Share the spinach, scallions, and diced tomatoes into 3 ramekins, gently stir, and assemble 3 slices of tomatoes on top in each ramekin.
2. Sprinkle with Parmesan cheese. Slightly place the ramekins in the pot, and seal the lid. Select "Manual" and cook on high pressure for 20 minutes. Once completed, quickly release the pressure.
3. Remove the ramekins carefully and use a paper towel to tap soak any water from the steam that sits on the quiche. Brown the top of the quiche using a fire torch.

## Nutrition

- Calories: 310
- Net carbs: 0 g.
- Fat: 27 g.
- Protein: 12 g.

# 50. Peas Soup

**Preparation time:** 10 minutes

**Cooking time:** 10 minutes

**Servings:** 4

## Ingredients

- 1 tbsp. olive oil
- 1 white onion, chopped
- 2 eggs
- 1-quart veggie stock
- 3 tbsps. lemon juice
- Salt and black pepper to the taste
- 2 tbsps. Parmesan, grated
- 2 c. peas

## Directions

1. Heat up a pot over medium-high heat with the oil, add the onion and sauté for 4 minutes.
2. Add the remaining ingredients except for the eggs, bring to a boil, and cook for 4 minutes.
3. Put the whisked eggs, stir the soup, cook for 2 minutes more, split into bowls, and serve.

## Nutrition

- Calories: 293
- Fiber: 3.4
- Fat: 11.2
- Protein: 4.45
- Carbs: 27

# 51. Steamed Artichokes

**Preparation time:** 5 minutes

**Cooking time:** 20 minutes

**Servings:** 3

## Ingredients

- 2 medium artichokes
- 3 lemon wedges (for cooking and serving)
- 1 ½ c. water

## Directions

1. Clean the artichokes by removing the stem, all dead leaves, and the top third of it. Rub the topmost of the artichokes with the lemon. Set aside. Place a trivet to fit in the Instant Pot, pour in water.
2. Place the artichokes on the trivet, seal the lid. Select Manual mode on High-Pressure for 9 minutes.
3. Once done, keep the pressure valve for 10 minutes; then rapidly release the remaining pressure.
4. Remove artichokes and serve with lemon wedges and garlic mayo.

## Nutrition

- Calories: 47
- Net carbs: 6 g.
- Protein: 3.3 g.
- Fat: 0.2 g.

## 52. Creamed Savoy Cabbage

**Preparation time:** 5 minutes

**Cooking time:** 15 minutes

**Servings:** 3

### Ingredients

- 2 small onions, chopped
- 2 medium savoy cabbages, finely chopped
- 2 ½ c. mixed bone Broth
- 2 c. bacon, chopped
- ¼ tsp. mace
- 1 bay leaf
- 2 c. coconut milk
- 3 tbsps. chopped parsley
- Salt to taste

### Directions

1. Set on Sauté. Add the onions and bacon crumbles; cook until crispy. Add bone broth and scrape the lowermost of the pot. Stir in cabbage and bay leaf. Cut out some parchment paper and cover the cabbage with it.
2. Seal the lid, choose Manual mode and cook on High-Pressure for about 4 minutes. Once completed, press Cancel and quickly release the pressure.
3. Select Sautee, stir in the nutmeg and milk. Simmer for 5 minutes then put the parsley.

### Nutrition

- Calories: 27
- Net carbs: 3.1 g.
- Fat: 3 g.
- Protein: 4 g.

## 53. Tilapia Delight

**Preparation time:** 6 minutes

**Cooking time:** 10 minutes

**Servings:** 4

### Ingredients

- 4 tbsps. lemon juice
- 4 tilapia fillets
- 2 tbsps. butter
- ½ c. parsley
- Salt and pepper, to taste
- 2 garlic cloves

### Directions

1. Melt butter on "Sauté," and add parsley and garlic cloves. Season with pepper and salt; stir well. Cook for 2–3 minutes. Then, add lemon juice and tilapia and stir well.
2. Seal the lid and set it on "Manual" mode. Cook for 10 minutes on high pressure.
3. When the timer beeps, allow the pressure to release naturally, for 5 minutes.

### Nutrition

- Calories: 135
- Fat: 4.4 g.
- Net carbs: 1.3 g.
- Protein: 23.7 g.

## 54. Spinach Tomatoes Mix

**Preparation time:** 4 minutes

**Cooking time:** 10 minutes

**Servings:** 2

### Ingredients

- 1 tbsp. butter
- 1 onion, chopped
- 2 cloves garlic, minced
- 1 tbsp. cumin powder
- 1 tbsp. Paprika
- 2 tomatoes, chopped
- 2 c. vegetable broth
- 1 small bunch of spinach, chopped
- Cilantro for garnishing

### Directions

1. Melt the butter on "Sauté" mode. Add garlic, cumin powder, onion, vegetable broth, and paprika, stir well. Add spinach and tomatoes and seal the lid, select "Manual" and cook on high pressure for 10 minutes.
2. When completed, do a quick pressure release.

### Nutrition

- Calories: 125
- Net carbs: 8.3 g.
- Fat: 5.5 g.
- Protein: 7.7 g.

## 55. Intermittent Buffalo Drumsticks and Chili Aioli

**Preparation time:** 12 minutes

**Cooking time:** 40 minutes

**Servings:** 6

## Ingredients

- 2 lbs. chicken drumsticks or chicken wings
- 2 tbsps. olive oil or coconut oil
- 2 tbsps. white wine vinegar
- 1 tbsp. tomato paste
- 1 tsp. salt
- 1 tsp. paprika powder
- 1 tbsp. Tabasco
- Butter or olive oil, for greasing the baking dish

## For the chili aioli:

- ⅔ c. mayonnaise
- 1 tbsp. smoked paprika powder or smoked chili powder
- 1 garlic clove, minced

## Directions

1. Preheat the oven to 450° (220°C).
2. Put the drumsticks in a plastic bag.
3. Mix the ingredients for the marinade and pour it into the plastic bag. Shake the bag and let marinate for 10 minutes.
4. Coat a baking dish with oil. Place the drumsticks in the baking bowl and let bake for 30–40 minutes or until they are done and have turned a beautiful color.
5. Mix together mayonnaise, garlic, and chili.

## Nutrition

- Calories: 409
- Protein: 22 g.
- Fat: 10 g.
- Net carbs: 6 g.

## 56. Cajun Blackened Fish With Cauliflower Salad

**Preparation time:** 9 minutes

**Cooking time:** 9 minutes

**Servings:** 1

### Ingredients

- 1 c. chopped cauliflower
- 1 tsp. red pepper flakes
- 1 tbsp. Italian seasonings
- 1 tbsp. garlic, minced
- 6 oz. tilapia
- 1 c. English cucumber, chopped with peel
- 2 tbsps. olive oil
- 1 sprig dill, chopped
- 1 sweetener packet
- 3 tbsps. lime juice
- 2 tbsps. Cajun blackened seasoning

### Directions

1. Mix the seasonings, except the Cajun blackened seasoning, into one bowl.
2. Add 1 tbsp. olive oil.
3. Emulsify or whip.
4. Pour the dressing over the cauliflower and cucumber.
5. Brush the fish with olive oil on both sides.
6. Pour the other 1 tbsp. oil into a coated skillet.
7. Press the Cajun seasoning onto both sides of the fish.
8. Cook the fish in olive oil for 3 minutes per side.
9. Plate and serve.

### Nutrition

- Calories: 530
- Total fat: 33.5 g.
- Protein: 32 g.
- Total carbs: 5.5 g.
- Dietary fiber: 4 g.
- Sugar: 3 g.

- Sodium: 80 mg.

# 57. Tuna Casserole

**Preparation time:** 20 minutes

**Cooking time:** 1 hour and 10 minutes

**Servings:** 9

## Ingredients

- ¼ c. avocado oil
- 1 onion, chopped
- 2 Zucchini, sliced
- 3 garlic cloves, minced
- 1 recipe cream of mushroom soup, cooled
- Zest of 1 lemon
- 1 tsp. dried dill
- 1 tbsp. Dijon mustard
- 1 lb. oil-packed tuna, drained
- 1 c. shredded Cheddar cheese

## Directions

1. Preheat the oven to 350°F.
2. Heat the oil over medium-high heat until it shimmers in a huge nonstick skillet. Add the zucchini and onion and cook, stirring rarely, until the veggies begin to soften, about 5 minutes.
3. Add the garlic and cook, stirring continuously for 30 seconds. Remove from the heat and cool.
4. Combine the lemon zest, cream of mushroom soup, mustard dill, in a huge bowl. Whisk until smooth. Add the tuna, cheese, and cooled vegetables. Mix to combine.
5. Spread into a 9x13-inch baking dish. Bake until bubbled, about 1 hour. Let cool.
6. Split the casserole between 9 storage containers.

## Nutrition

- Calories: 761
- Net carbs: 9 g.

- Protein: 53 g.
- Total fat: 59 g.
- Fiber: 3 g.
- Total carbs: 12 g.
- Sodium: 473 mg.

## 58. Cheesy Chicken and Mushroom Casserole

**Preparation time:** 20 minutes

**Cooking time:** 1 hour and 15 minutes

**Servings:** 8

### Ingredients

- 8 bone-in chicken thighs
- 1 lb. button mushrooms, halved
- 1 (8 oz.) bag of frozen pearl onions
- 1 recipe cream of mushroom Soup, cooled
- 1 c. shredded Cheddar cheese

### Directions

- Preheat the oven to 350°F.
- Arrange the mushrooms, chicken thighs, and onions in a 9-by-13-inch baking dish, so they are well mixed but spread all over the pan.
- In a bowl, stir the cheese and soup together. Pour over the mushrooms, onions, and chicken.
- Cover with aluminum foil, bake for 1 hour and 15 minutes, or until the chicken is its juices run clear and cooked through. Let cool.
- Split the casserole between 8 storage containers.

### Nutrition

- Calories: 609
- Protein: 25 g.
- Total fat: 56 g.
- Net carbs: 9 g.
- Sodium: 383 mg.

- Total carbs: 11 g.
- Fiber: 2 g.

## 59. Pork Burrito Bowls

**Preparation time:** 15 minutes, plus 4–8 hours to marinate

**Cooking time:** 20 minutes

**Servings:** 4

### Ingredients

- ½ c. avocado oil, divided
- Juice of 3 limes
- 1 bunch fresh cilantro, leaves chopped
- 1 jalapeño pepper, minced
- 6 garlic cloves, minced
- ½ tsp. salt
- 6 scallions, both white and green parts, finely minced
- 1 lb. pork belly
- 1 onion, sliced
- 2 c. cooked cauliflower rice
- 1 green bell pepper, thinly sliced
- ½ c. sour cream
- 1 avocado, halved, pitted, and chopped
- 1 c. shredded cheddar cheese

### Directions

1. Whisk together ¼ c. the oil, the cilantro, lime juice, jalapeño, salt, scallions, and garlic in a medium bowl. Set aside 2 tbsps. the mixture.
2. Place the remaining mixture in a large zip-top bag and put the pork belly. Coat the meat with the marinade, seal the bag, and put it in a refrigerator for 4–8 hours.
3. In a huge skillet, heat the remaining ¼ c. oil on over medium-high heat until it shimmers.
4. Remove the meat from the marinade and wipe away any excess. Cook it in the hot oil until it reaches an internal temperature of 145°F, about 5 minutes per side. Set aside on a platter, tented with foil, to rest.
5. Add the onion and bell pepper using the same skillet. Cook, stirring occasionally, until the veggies are soft, about 5 minutes.
6. Slice the meat thinly against the grain and put it back in the pan. Add the reserved 2 tbsps. marinade. Cook, stirring, for 2 minutes, or until the veggies and meat are coated with the marinade.

7. Divide the sliced pork and vegetables into 4 storage containers, Place ½ c. cauliflower rice into each of 4 separate storage containers. To serve, mix the veggies, meat, and cauliflower rice together and top with sour cream, avocado, and cheese.

## Nutrition

- Calories: 528
- Protein: 41 g.
- Total fat: 35 g.
- Sodium: 474 mg.
- Net carbs: 12 g.
- Total carbs: 18 g.
- Fiber: 6 g.

# 60. Slow Cooker Pork Chili

**Preparation time:** 15 minutes

**Cooking time:** 4–8 hours

**Servings:** 8

## Ingredients

- 1 onion, chopped
- 2 lbs. boneless pork shoulder, cut into cubes
- 3 tbsps. chili powder
- 1 tsp. garlic powder
- 1 tsp. salt
- 1 tsp. ground coriander
- 1 tsp. ground cumin
- 1 c. sour cream
- 1 c. shredded Cheddar cheese

## Directions

1. Combine the onion, pork shoulder, coriander, cumin, chili powder, salt, and garlic powder in a huge slow cooker.
2. Stir to mix. Cover it and cook on high for 4 hours or on low for 8 hours. Let it cool.
3. Place 1 ½ c. chili into each of 8 storage containers.
4. To serve, garnish with sour cream and cheese.

## Nutrition

- Calories: 466
- Protein: 31 g.
- Total fat: 36 g.
- Net carbs: 4 g.
- Total carbs: 5 g.
- Sodium: 268 mg.
- Fiber: 1 g.

# 61. Pork Stir-Fry

**Preparation time:** 15 minutes

**Cooking time:** 10 minutes

**Servings:** 6

## Ingredients

- 1 lb. ground pork
- 3 tbsps. coconut oil
- 6 scallions
- 1 tbsp. grated peeled fresh ginger
- 2 c. shredded green cabbage or bagged coleslaw mix
- 3 garlic cloves, minced
- 1 tbsp. low-sodium soy sauce
- Juice of 2 limes
- ½ tsp. chili oil
- ½ tsp. sesame oil

## Directions

1. Heat the coconut oil over medium-high heat in a huge skillet until it shimmers.
2. Put the pork and cook, stirring, until it just begins to brown, about 5 minutes.
3. Add the cabbage, ginger, and scallions. Cook till the vegetables are soft, about 3 minutes more.
4. Add the garlic and cook, stirring continuously, for about 30 seconds.
5. Add the soy sauce, lime juice, chili oil, sesame oil, and cook for 1–2 minutes, or until heated through.
6. Split the stir-fry between 6 storage containers.

## Nutrition

- Calories: 698
- Protein: 54 g.
- Total fat: 50 g.
- Net carbs: 4 g.
- Sodium: 367 mg.
- Total carbs: 5 g.
- Fiber: 1 g.

## 62. Chicken Parmesan Over Protein: Pasta

**Preparation time:** 9 minutes

**Cooking time:** 14 minutes

**Servings:** 2

### Ingredients

- 1 dash black pepper
- ½ tsp. Italian spice mix
- 8 oz. protein plus spaghetti
- ½ hand-shredded Parmesan
- 1 diced zucchini squash
- 1 ½ c. marinara sauce, any brand
- 24 oz. boneless thin chicken cutlets
- 2 tbsps. olive oil
- ½ c. grated Mozzarella cheese
- Water, for boiling the pasta

### Directions

1. Boil the pasta with the zucchini in the water.
2. Mix the Italian spices and ¼ c. Parmesan cheese and place in a shallow dish.
3. Brush the chicken pieces with olive oil and press into spice and cheese to coat.
4. Place in skillet with the oil and cook until done.
5. Add the marinara sauce to the skillet to warm, cover the chicken if you desire.
6. Drain the pasta and zucchini, place on plates.
7. Top the chicken with the Mozzarella and the remaining Parmesan cheese.
8. Place sauce, chicken, and cheese onto the spaghetti and serve.

### Nutrition

- Calories: 372
- Total fat: 18 g.
- Protein: 56 g.
- Total carbs: 7 g.
- Dietary fiber: 2 g.
- Sugar: 6 g.
- Sodium: 1335 mg.

# 63. Chicken Chow Mein Stir Fry

**Preparation time:** 9 minutes

**Cooking time:** 14 minutes

**Servings:** 4

## Ingredients

- ½ c. sliced onion
- 2 tbsps. oil, sesame garlic flavored
- 4 c. shredded bok choy
- 1 c. sugar snap peas
- 1 c. fresh bean sprouts
- 3 stalks celery, chopped
- 1 ½ tsp. minced garlic
- 1 packet Splenda
- 1 c. broth, chicken
- 2 tbsps. soy sauce
- 1 tbsp. ginger, freshly minced
- 1 tsp. cornstarch
- 4 boneless chicken breasts, cooked/sliced thinly

## Directions

1. Place the bok choy, peas, celery in a skillet with 1 tbsp. garlic oil.
2. Stir fry until bok choy is softened to liking.
3. Add the remaining ingredients except for the cornstarch.
4. If too thin, stir cornstarch into ½ c. cold water. When smooth pour into skillet.
5. Bring cornstarch and chow mein to a 1-minute boil. Turn off the heat source.
6. Stir sauce, then wait 4 minutes to serve, after the chow mein has thickened.

## Nutrition

- Calories: 368
- Total fat: 18 g.
- Protein: 42 g.
- Total carbs: 12 g.
- Dietary fiber: 16 g.
- Sugar: 6 g.
- Sodium: 746 mg.

# 64. Colorful Chicken Casserole

**Preparation time:** 14 minutes

**Cooking time:** 14 minutes

**Servings:** 6

## Ingredients

- 1 c. broth, chicken
- 3 c. cooked chicken, diced
- 4 c. chopped broccoli
- 1 c. assorted colored bell peppers, chopped
- 1 c. cream
- 4 tbsps. sherry
- ¼ c. hand-shredded Parmesan cheese
- 1 small size can of black olives, sliced, drained
- 2 tortilla Factory low-carb whole wheat tortillas
- ½ c. hand-shredded Mozzarella

## Directions

1. Place broccoli and chicken broth into a skillet.
2. Top with lid, bring to a boil, and steam until desired crispness. (4 min)
3. Add the peppers, steam for one minute if you don't want them crisp.
4. Add the chicken and stir to heat.
5. Combine the sherry, cream, Parmesan, and olives.
6. Tear the tortillas into bite-sized pieces.
7. Stir into the chicken and broccoli.
8. Pour cream sauce over the chicken, stir.
9. Top with hand-shredded Mozzarella.
10. Broil in the oven until cheese is melted and golden brown.

## Nutrition

- Calories: 412
- Total fat: 30 g.
- Protein: 29
- Total carbs: 10 g.
- Dietary fiber: 9 g.
- Sugar: 1 g.
- Sodium: 712 mg.

## 65. Chives Trout

**Preparation time:** 10 minutes

**Cooking time:** 12 minutes

**Servings:** 4

## Ingredients

- 4 trout fillets, boneless
- 2 shallots, chopped
- A pinch of salt and black pepper
- 3 tbsps. chives, chopped
- 2 tbsps. avocado oil
- 2 tsps. lime juice

## Directions

1. Ensure that you heat the pan, add the shallots and sauté them for 2 minutes.
2. Add the fish and the rest of the ingredients cook for 5 minutes on each side, divide between plates and serve.

## Nutrition

- Calories: 320
- Fat: 12 g.
- Fiber: 1 g.
- Carbs: 2 g.
- Protein: 24 g.

## 66. Salmon and Tomatoes

**Preparation time:** 10 minutes

**Cooking time:** 25 minutes

**Servings:** 4

### Ingredients

- 2 tbsps. avocado oil
- 4 salmon fillets, boneless
- 1 c. cherry tomatoes, halved
- 2 spring onions, chopped
- ½ c. chicken stock
- A pinch of salt and black pepper
- ½ tsp. rosemary, dried

### Directions

1. In a roasting pan, combine the fish with the oil and the other ingredients, introduce it in the oven at 400°F and bake for 25 minutes.
2. Divide between plates and serve.

### Nutrition

- Calories: 200
- Fat: 12 g.
- Fiber: 0 g.
- Carbs: 3 g.
- Protein: 21 g.

# 67. Herb Butter Scallops

**Preparation time:** 10 minutes

**Cooking time:** 10 minutes

**Servings:**3

## Ingredients

- 1 lb. sea scallops, cleaned
- Freshly ground black pepper
- 8 tbsps. butter, divided
- 2 tsps. minced garlic
- Juice of 1 lemon
- 2 tsps. chopped fresh basil
- 1 tsp. chopped fresh thyme

## Directions

1. Pat the scallops dry with paper towels and put some pepper.
2. Place a huge skillet over medium heat and put 2 tbsps. butter.
3. Arrange the scallops in the skillet, evenly spaced but not too near together, and sear each side till they are golden brown, about 2 ½ minutes per side.
4. Remove the scallops to a plate and set them aside.
5. Put the remaining 6 tbsps. butter into the skillet and sauté the garlic until translucent, about 3 minutes.
6. Stir in the thyme, lemon juice, and basil, and put the scallops back to the skillet, turning to coat them in the sauce.
7. Serve.

## Nutrition

- Calories: 306
- Protein: 19 g.
- Fat: 24 g.
- Fiber: 0 g.
- Carbohydrates: 4 g.

# 68. Cilantro-Lime Flounder

**Preparation time:** 20 minutes

**Cooking time:** 6 minutes

**Servings:** 3

## Ingredients

- ¼ c. homemade mayonnaise
- 1 lime juice zest
- ½ c. fresh cilantro
- 3 (3 oz.) flounder fillets

## Directions

1. Set the oven to 300°F. Stir the lime juice, mayonnaise, cilantro, and lime zest in a small bowl. Place 3 pieces of foil on a clean work surface, about 8x8-inch square. Place a flounder fillet in the center of each square.
2. Top the fillets evenly with the mixture of mayonnaise. Add pepper to the flounder. Fold the foil sides over the fish, create a snug packet, and place on a baking sheet the foil packets. Bake the fish for 3–6 minutes. Unfold and display the boxes.

## Nutrition

- Fat: 3 g.
- Protein: 12 g.
- Phosphorus: 208 mg.
- Carbohydrates: 2 g.
- Sodium: 268 mg.
- Potassium: 138 mg.

# 69. Seafood Casserole

**Preparation time:** 20 minutes

**Cooking time:** 36 minutes

**Servings:** 6

## Ingredients

- Sliced and cut in 1-inch bits of butter
- 2 c. eggplant
- 1 tbsp. olive oil
- 1 tbsp. minced garlic
- ½ small sweet onion
- 1 celery stalk
- 3 tbsps. freshly squeezed lemon juice
- ½ red bell pepper
- 1 tbsp. hot sauce
- ½ c. white rice
- 1 large egg
- ¼ tbsps. creole seasoning mix
- High 3 oz. cooked shrimp.

## Directions

1. Cook the eggplant for about 6 minutes in a small saucepan filled with water over medium-high heat. Drain in a huge bowl and set aside.
2. Grease and set aside an 8x13-inch butter baking dish. Heat the olive oil in a large pot over medium heat.
3. Drizzle the garlic, onion, pepper bell, and celery, for about 3 minutes or until tender. In addition to the hot sauce, lemon juice, Creole seasoning, egg, and rice and add the sautéed vegetables to the eggplant.
4. Remove to combine. Fold in the meat of the crab and shrimp.
5. Spoon the casserole mixture in the casserole dish, and pat down the top. Bake for 26–40 minutes till the casserole is heated through and the rice is tender. Serve hot.

## Nutrition

- Fat: 3 g
- Protein: 12 g.
- Phosphorus: 102 mg.

- Sodium: 236 mg.
- Carbohydrates: 8 g
- Potassium: 188 mg.

# 70. Herb Pesto Tuna

**Preparation time:** 10 minutes

**Cooking time:** 10 minutes

**Servings:** 3

## Ingredients

- 1 tbsp. olive oil
- 3 (3 oz.) yellowfin tuna fillets
- Freshly ground black pepper
- 1 lemon, cut into 8 thin slices
- ¼ c. herb pesto

## Directions

1. Heat to medium-high barbecue.
2. Add the olive oil to the fish and dust each fillet with pepper.
3. On the barbeque, cook it for 3 minutes.
4. Turn over the fish and top each piece using the herb slices.
5. Grill until the tuna is cooked to medium-well for 6–6 minutes longer.

## Nutrition

- Fat: 2 g
- Sodium: 38 mg.
- Phosphorus: 236 mg.

## 71. Grilled Calamari With Lemon and Herbs

**Preparation time:** 10 minutes

**Cooking time:** 3 minutes

**Servings:** 3

### Ingredients

- 2 tbsps. freshly squeezed lemon juice
- ½ lb. calamari
- 2 tbsps. olive oil
- 1 tbsp. chopped fresh parsley
- 2 tbsps. minced garlic
- 1 tbsp. chopped fresh oregano

### Directions

1. Combine lemon juice, olive oil, oregano, garlic, petroleum, salt, and pepper in a large bowl.
2. In the bowl, add the calamari and stir to coat.
3. Cover the bowl and cool the calamari to marinate for 1 hour. Preheat to medium-high the barbecue.
4. Grill the calamari for about 3 minutes, turning once, until opaque and firm. Serve with lemon wedges.

### Nutrition

- Fat: 8 g
- Phosphorus: 128 mg.
- Carbohydrates: 2 g.
- Potassium: 160 mg.
- Protein: 3 g
- Sodium: 68 mg.

# 72. Traditional Chicken-Vegetable Soup

**Preparation time:** 20 minutes

**Cooking time:** 36 minutes

## Ingredients

- ½ sweet onion
- 1 tbsp. unsalted butter
- 2 tbsps. chopped garlic
- 1 carrot chopped
- 2 celery stalks
- 1 c. easy chicken stock
- 2 c. chicken breast chopped
- 3 c. water
- 1 tbsp. freshly chopped thyme
- Black pepper freshly ground
- 2 tbsps. chopped fresh parsley

## Directions

1. Melt the butter in a huge pot over medium heat.
2. Sauté the garlic and onion for about 3 minutes until softened.
3. Add carrot, celery, stuffed chicken, chicken, and water.
4. Bring the soup to a boil, reduce heat, and boil until the vegetables are tender for about 40 minutes.
5. Put the thyme and cook the soup for 2 minutes.
6. Dust with pepper and serve with parsley on top.

## Nutrition

- Fat: 6 g.
- Phosphorus: 108 mg.
- Carbohydrates: 2 g
- Potassium: 188 mg.
- Protein: 16 g
- Sodium: 62 mg.

## 73. Arroz con Pollo

**Preparation time:** 15 minutes

**Cooking time:** 20 minutes

**Servings:** 4

### Ingredients

- 1 lb. boneless, skinless chicken thighs, chopped
- ¼ c. avocado oil
- 1 onion, chopped
- 1 (14 oz.) can crushed tomatoes, with their juices
- 8 oz. mushrooms, sliced
- 1 tbsp. chili powder
- 1 tsp. ground cumin
- 1 tsp. dried oregano
- 1 tsp. garlic powder
- Pinch cayenne pepper
- ½ tsp. salt
- 2 c. uncooked cauliflower rice
- ½ c. sour cream, for garnish
- 1 c. shredded Monterey Jack cheese

### Directions

1. Heat the avocado oil over medium-high in a huge nonstick skillet, until it shimmers.
2. Put the chicken and cook, stirring occasionally, until it is browned, about 5 minutes. Remove the chicken from the oil using a slotted spoon, and set it aside.
3. Add the mushrooms and onion to the skillet. Cook, stirring rarely until the vegetables are browned, about 5 minutes.
4. Put the chicken back to the skillet with the vegetables, adding any juices that have collected on the plate.
5. Add the chili powder, tomatoes and their juices, oregano, cayenne, garlic powder, cumin, and salt, and bring to a boil, stirring.
6. Put the cauliflower. Cook, stirring occasionally, for 5 minutes.
7. Add the cheese. Cook, stirring, just until the cheese melts and mixes in, about 2 minutes more.
8. Divide the chicken and cauliflower rice into 4 containers. To serve, garnish with sour cream.

## Nutrition

- Calories: 513
- Protein: 31 g.
- Total fat: 35 g.
- Net carbs: 13 g.
- Sodium: 687 mg.
- Total carbs: 20 g.
- Fiber: 7 g.

## 74. Pan-Seared Halibut With Citrus Butter Sauce

**Preparation time:** 10 minutes

**Cooking time:** 15 minutes

**Servings:** 3

### Ingredients

- Sea salt
- 4 (5 oz.) halibut fillets, each about 1-inch thick
- Freshly ground black pepper
- 2 tsps. minced garlic
- ¼ c. butter
- 1 shallot, minced
- 2 tbsps. dry white wine
- 1 tbsp. freshly squeezed lemon juice
- 1 tbsp. freshly squeezed orange juice
- 1 tsps. chopped fresh parsley
- 1 tbsp. olive oil

### Directions

1. Pat the fish dry with paper towels and then season the fillets with pepper and salt. Set aside on a paper towel-lined plate.
2. Place a small saucepan over medium heat and melt the butter.
3. Sauté the shallot and garlic until tender, about 3 minutes.

4. Whisk in the lemon juice, white wine, and orange juice and bring the sauce to a boil, cooking until it thickens a little, about 2 minutes.
5. Remove the sauce from the heat and stir in the parsley; set aside.
6. Place a huge skillet over medium-high heat and put the olive oil.
7. Panfry the fish until lightly browned and just cooked through, turning them over once, about 10 minutes in total.
8. Serve the fish instantly with a spoonful of sauce for each.

## Nutrition

- Calories: 319
- Protein: 22 g.
- Fat: 26 g.
- Fiber: 0 g.
- Carbohydrates: 2 g.

## 75. Salmon and Coconut Mix

**Preparation time:** 10 minutes

**Cooking time:** 20 minutes

**Servings:** 4

### Ingredients

- 4 salmon fillets, boneless
- 3 tbsps. avocado mayonnaise
- 1 tsp. lime zest, grated
- ¼ c. coconut cream
- ¼ c. lime juice
- ½ c. coconut, unsweetened and shredded
- 2 tsps. Cajun seasoning
- A pinch of salt
- Pinch of black pepper

### Directions

1. Place the Instant Pot on "Sauté" mode, put the coconut cream and the rest of the ingredients except the fish, mix and cook for at least 5 minutes.
2. Add the fish, set the lid on, and cook on high for at least 10 minutes.
3. Release the pressure for 10 minutes, split the salmon and sauce between plates, and serve.

### Nutrition

- Calories: 306
- Protein: 25.3 g.
- Fiber: 1.4 g.
- Fat: 17.5 g.
- Carbs: 2.5 g.

# 76. Tilapia and Red Sauce

**Preparation time:** 10 minutes

**Cooking time:** 20 minutes

**Servings:** 4

## Ingredients

- A pinch of salt and black pepper
- 4 tilapia fillets, boneless
- 2 tbsps. avocado oil
- 2 spring onions, minced
- 1 tbsp. lemon juice
- ½ c. chicken stock
- 1 tsp. garlic powder
- ¼ c. tomato passata
- 1 tsp. oregano, dried
- 10 oz. canned tomatoes and chilies, chopped
- 1 c. roasted red peppers, chopped

## Directions

1. Set the Instant Pot on "Sauté" mode, heat up the oil, put the onions, and cook for 2 minutes.
2. Put the rest of the ingredients excluding the fish, and boil everything for 8 minutes more.
3. Put the fish, set the lid on, and cook on high for 10 minutes.
4. Release the pressure naturally for 10 minutes, split everything between plates, and serve.

## Nutrition

- Calories: 184
- Protein: 22.2 g.
- Fat: 2.2 g.
- Carbs: 1.9 g.
- Fiber: 1.6 g.

# 77. Lime Cod Mix

**Preparation time:** 10 minutes

**Cooking time:** 15 minutes

**Servings:** 4

## Ingredients

- ½ tsp. cumin, ground
- 4 cod fillets, boneless
- 1 tbsp. olive oil
- A pinch of salt and black pepper
- ½ c. chicken stock
- 2 tbsps. lime juice
- 2 tsps. lime zest, grated
- 3 tbsps. cilantro, chopped

## Directions

1. Set the Instant Pot on "Sauté" mode, heat the oil, add the cod, and cook for 1 minute on each side.
2. Add the remaining ingredients, put the lid on, and cook on high for 13 minutes.
3. Release the pressure naturally for around 10 minutes, split the mix between plates, and serve.

## Nutrition

- Calories: 187
- Fiber: 0.2 g.
- Fat: 13.1 g.
- Protein: 16.1 g.
- Carbs: 1.6 g.

## 78. Sole Asiago

**Preparation time:** 10 minutes

**Cooking time:** 8 minutes

**Servings:** 4

## Ingredients

- 4 (4 oz.) sole fillets
- ¾ c. ground almonds
- ¼ c. Asiago cheese
- 2 eggs, beaten
- 2 ½ tbsps. melted coconut oil

## Directions

1. Preheat the oven to 350°F. Line a baking sheet with parchment paper and set it aside.
2. Pat the fish dry using paper towels.
3. Combine the ground almonds and cheese in a small bowl.
4. Place the bowl with the beaten eggs next to the almond mixture.
5. Dredge a sole fillet in the beaten egg and then place the fish into the almond mixture so it is completely coated. Place on the baking sheet and repeat until all the fillets are breaded.
6. Brush both sides of each piece of fish with coconut oil.
7. Bake the sole until it is cooked through, about 8 minutes in total.
8. Serve.

## Nutrition

- Calories: 406
- Protein: 29 g.
- Fat: 31 g.
- Fiber: 3 g.
- Carbohydrates: 6 g.

## 79. Cheesy Garlic Salmon

**Preparation time:** 15 minutes

**Cooking time:** 12 minutes

**Servings:**4

### Ingredients

- 2 tbsps. freshly squeezed lemon juice
- ½ c. Asiago cheese
- 4 (5 oz.) salmon fillets
- 2 tbsps. butter, at room temperature
- 1 tsp. chopped fresh basil
- 2 tsps. minced garlic
- 1 tbsp. olive oil
- 1 tsp. chopped fresh oregano

### Directions

1. Preheat the oven to 350°F. Line a baking sheet with parchment paper and set it aside.
2. Stir together the lemon juice, Asiago cheese, garlic, butter, oregano, and basil in a small bowl.
3. Pat the salmon dry with paper towels and place the fillets on the baking sheet skin-side down. Split the topping evenly between the fillets and spread it across the fish by using the back of a spoon or knife.
4. Sprinkle the fish with the olive oil and bake until the topping is golden and the fish is just cooked through about 12 minutes.
5. Serve.

### Nutrition

- Calories: 357
- Protein: 24 g.
- Fat: 28 g.
- Fiber: 0 g.
- Carbohydrates: 2 g.

# 80. Stuffed Chicken Breasts

**Preparation time:** 30 minutes

**Cooking time:** 30 minutes

**Servings:** 4

## Ingredients

- ¼ c. chopped sweet onion
- 1 tbsp. butter
- ¼ c. chopped roasted red pepper
- ¼ c. Kalamata olives, chopped
- ½ c. goat cheese, at room temperature
- 1 tbsp. chopped fresh basil
- 1 (5 oz.) chicken breasts, skin-on
- 2 tbsps. extra-virgin olive oil

## Directions

1. Preheat the oven to 400°F.
2. Melt the butter in a small skillet over medium heat and add the onion. Sauté until tender, about 3 minutes.
3. Transfer the onion to a medium bowl and add the olives, cheese, basil, and red pepper. Stir until well blended, then refrigerate for about 30 minutes.
4. Cut horizontal pockets into each chicken breast, and stuff them evenly with the filling. Secure the two sides of each breast with toothpicks.
5. Place a huge ovenproof skillet over medium-high heat and add the olive oil.
6. Brown the chicken on both sides, about 10 minutes in total.
7. Place the skillet in the oven and roast until the chicken is just cooked through, about 15 minutes. Remove the toothpicks and serve.

## Nutrition

- Calories: 389
- Protein: 25 g.
- Fat: 30 g.
- Fiber: 0 g.
- Carbohydrates: 3 g.

## 81. Chicken Relleno Casserole

**Preparation time:** 19 minutes

**Cooking time:** 29 minutes

**Servings:** 6

### Ingredients

- 6 tortilla factory low-carb whole wheat tortillas, torn into small pieces
- 1 ½ c. hand-shredded cheese, Mexican
- 1 beaten egg
- 1 c. milk
- 2 c. cooked chicken, shredded
- 1 can of Ro-Tel
- ½ c. Salsa Verde

### Directions

1. Grease an 8x8-inch glass baking dish.
2. Heat the oven to 375°F.
3. Combine everything together, but reserve ½ c. the cheese.
4. Bake it for 29 minutes.
5. Take it out of the oven and add ½ c. cheese.
6. Broil for about 2 minutes to melt the cheese.

### Nutrition

- Calories: 265
- Total fat: 16 g.
- Protein: 20 g.
- Total carbs: 18 g.
- Dietary fiber: 10 g.
- Sugar: 0 g.
- Sodium: 708 mg.

## 82. Italian Chicken With Asparagus and Artichoke Hearts

**Preparation time:** 9 minutes

**Cooking time:** 40 minutes

**Servings:** 1

## Ingredients

- 1 can long asparagus spears, drained
- 1 c. red peppers, roasted, drained
- 1 c. artichoke hearts, drained
- 6 oz. boneless chicken breast, pounded thin or sliced thinly
- 2 tbsps. Parmesan cheese
- 1 tbsp. bisquick
- ½ tsp. oregano
- ½ tsp. garlic powder
- ½ c. fresh sliced mushrooms
- 2 tbsps. red wine vinegar
- 2 tbsps. butter
- 3 tbsps. olive oil

## Directions

1. Place in a small blender container (or bowl) the oregano, garlic powder, vinegar, and 1 tbsp. oil. Place it to the side.
2. Combine the bisquick and Parmesan cheese.
3. Roll the chicken in the bisquick and Parmesan mix.
4. Heat the butter in a skillet.
5. Brown the chicken on both sides and cook until done for approximately 4 minutes.
6. Emulsify or quickly whip the wet ingredients you have placed to the side. This is your dressing.
7. Place the chicken on the plate.
8. Surround with the vegetables and drizzle them with the dressing.

## Nutrition

- Calories: 435
- Total fat: 18 g.
- Protein: 38 g.
- Total carbs: 16 g.

- Dietary fiber: 7 g.
- Sugar: 1 g.
- Sodium: 860 mg.

## 83. Kabobs With Peanut Curry Sauce

**Preparation time:** 9 minutes

**Cooking time:** 9 minutes

**Servings:** 4

### Ingredients

- 1 c. cream
- 4 tsps. curry powder
- 1 ½ tsp. cumin
- 1 ½ tsp. salt
- 1 tbsp. minced garlic
- ⅓ c. peanut butter, sugar-free
- 2 tbsps. lime juice
- 3 tbsps. water
- ½ small onion, diced
- 2 tbsps. soy sauce
- 1 packet Splenda
- 8 oz. boneless, cooked chicken breast
- 8 oz. pork tenderloin

### Directions

- Blend together cream, onion, 2 tsps. garlic, curry and cumin powder, and salt.
- Slice the meats into 1-inch pieces.
- Place the cream sauce into a bowl and put the chicken and tenderloin to marinate. Let rest in the sauce for 14 minutes.
- Blend peanut butter, water, 1 tsp. garlic, lime juice, soy sauce, and Splenda. This is your peanut dipping sauce.
- Remove the meats and thread on skewers. Broil or grill 4 minutes per side until meat is done.
- Serve with dipping sauce.

### Nutrition

- Calories: 530
- Total fat: 29 g.
- Protein: 37 g.

- Total carbs: 6 g.
- Dietary fiber: 4 g.
- Sugar: 2 g.
- Sodium: 1538 mg.

# 84. Intermittent Fish Casserole

**Preparation time:** 10 minutes

**Cooking time:** 20 minutes

**Servings:** 4

## Ingredients

- 2 tbsps. olive oil
- 15 oz. broccoli
- 6 scallions
- 2 tbsps. small capers
- ⅙ oz. butter, for greasing the casserole dish
- 25 oz. white fish, in serving-sized pieces
- 1¼ c. heavy whipping cream
- 1 tbsp. Dijon mustard
- 1 tsp. salt
- ¼ tsp. ground black pepper
- 1 tbsp. dried parsley
- 3 oz. butter

## Directions

1. Preheat the oven to 400°F.
2. Divide the broccoli into smaller floret heads and include the stems. Peel it with a sharp knife or a potato peeler if the stem is rough or leafy.
3. Fry the broccoli florets in oil on medium-high heat for about 5 minutes, until they are golden and soft. Season with salt and pepper to taste.
4. Add finely chopped scallions and the capers. Fry this for another 1–2 minutes and place the vegetables in a baking dish that has been greased.
5. Place the fish tightly in amongst the vegetables.
6. Mix the parsley, whipping cream, and mustard together. Pour this over the fish and vegetables. Top it with slices of butter.
7. Bake the fish until it is cooked through, and it flakes easily with a fork. Serve as is, or with a tasty green salad.

## Nutrition

- Calories: 314
- Protein: 20 g.

- Fat: 8 g.
- Net carbs: 5 g.

## 85. Slow Cooker Intermittent Pork Roast

**Preparation time:** 35 minutes

**Cooking time:** 8 hours 20 minutes

**Servings:** 4

### Ingredients

- 30 oz. pork shoulder or pork roast
- ½ tbsp. salt
- 1 bay leaf
- 5 black pep
- ½ tbsp peppercorns
- 2 ½ c. water
- 2 tsps. dried thyme or dried rosemary
- 2 garlic cloves
- 1 ½ oz. fresh ginger
- 1 tbsp. olive oil or coconut oil
- 1 tbsp. paprika powder
- ½ tsp. ground black pepper

### For the creamy gravy:

- 1 ½ c. heavy whipping cream
- Juices from the roast

### Directions

1. Preheat the oven to low heat of 200°F.
2. Season the meat with salt and place it into a deep baking dish.
3. Add water. Add a bay leaf, peppercorns, and thyme for more seasoning. Place the baking bowl in the oven for 7–8 hours and cover it with aluminum foil.
4. If you are using a slow cooker for this, do the same process as in step 2 only add 1 c. water. Cook it for 8 hours on low or for 4 hours on a high setting.

5. Take the meat out of the baking dish, and reserve the pan juices in a separate pan to make gravy.
6. Turn the oven up to 450°F.
7. Finely chop or press the garlic and ginger into a small bowl. Add the oil, herbs, and pepper and stir well to combine them together.
8. Rub the meat with the garlic and herb mixture.
9. Return the meat back to the baking dish, and roast it for about 10–15 minutes or until it looks golden-brown.
10. Cut the meat into thin slices to serve it with the creamy gravy and a fibrous vegetable side dish.

## To make the gravy:

1. Strain the reserved pan juices to get rid of any solid pieces from the liquid. Boil and reduce the pan juices to about half the original volume, this should be about 1 c.
2. Pour the reduction into a pot with whipping cream. Bring this to a boil. Reduce the heat and let it simmer to your desired consistency for a creamy gravy.

## Nutrition

- Calories: 432
- Protein: 15 g.
- Fat: 29 g.
- Net carbs: 13 g

# Dinner

**86.** **Spicy Intermittent Chicken Wings**

**Preparation time:** 20 minutes

**Cooking time:** 30 minutes

**Servings:** 4

## Ingredients

- 2 lbs. chicken wings
- 1 tsp. Cajun spice
- 2 tsps. smoked paprika
- 50 tsps. turmeric
- Dash salt
- 2 tsps. baking powder
- Dash pepper

## Directions

1. Heat the stove to 400°F.
2. Dry the chicken wings with a paper towel to remove any excess moisture and get you some nice, crispy wings!
3. Get a mixing bowl and place all of the seasonings along with the baking powder. You can adjust the seasoning levels however you would like.
4. Coat the chicken wings. You can place the wings on a wire rack that is placed over your baking tray if you have one. If not, you can just lay them across the baking sheet.
5. Once the chicken wings are set, pop them into the stove for 30 minutes. The tops of the wings should be crispy.
6. Take them out from the oven and flip them so that you can bake the other side then cook for an additional 30 minutes.
7. Remove the tray from the oven and cool slightly before serving. Serve with any of your desired intermittent-friendly dipping sauce.

## Nutrition

- Fat: 7 g.
- Carbs: 1 g.
- Protein: 60 g.

## 87. Cheesy Ham Quiche

**Preparation time:** 10 minutes

**Cooking time:** 30 minutes

**Servings:** 6

### Ingredients

- 8 eggs
- 1 c. zucchini
- 50 c. shredded heavy cream
- 1 c. ham, diced
- 1 tsp. mustard
- Dash salt

### Directions

1. Prepare your stove to 375°F. and get a pie plate for your quiche.
2. Shred the zucchini into small pieces.
3. Get a paper towel and gently squeeze out the excess moisture to avoid a soggy quiche.
4. Place the Zucchini into a pie plate along with the cheese and cooked ham pieces.
5. Whisk the cream, seasonings, and eggs together before pouring them over the top.
6. Pop the dish into your stove for about 40 minutes.
7. The egg should be cooked through, and you will be able to insert a knife into the middle and have it come out clean.

8. Take the dish from the oven and allow it to chill slightly before slicing and serving.

## Nutrition

- Fat: 25 g.
- Protein: 20 g.
- Carbs: 2 g.

# 88. Feta and Cauliflower Rice Stuffed Bell Peppers

**Preparation time:** 10 minutes

**Cooking time:** 20 minutes

**Servings:** 3

## Ingredients

- 1 onion, sliced
- 1 red bell pepper
- 1 green bell pepper
- 1 yellow bell pepper
- 1 c. Feta cheese
- ½ c. cauliflower rice
- 1 tomato, chopped

237

- 1 tbsp. black pepper
- 2–3 garlic cloves, minced
- 1 tbsp. lemon juice
- 3–4 green olives, chopped
- 3–4 tbsps. olive oil

## For the yogurt sauce:

- 1 garlic clove, pressed
- 1 c. Greek yogurt
- 2 kosher salt, to taste
- juice from 1 lemon
- 2 tbsps. fresh dill

## Directions

1. Put olive oil in the Instant Pot. Cut at the topmost of the bell peppers near the stem. Place onion, feta cheese, olives, cauliflower rice, tomatoes, lemon juice, garlic powder, salt, black pepper, and into a bowl; mix well.
2. Fill up the bell peppers with the feta mixture and set the Instant Pot. Set on "Manual" and cook on high pressure for 20 minutes. When the timer beeps, allow the pressure to release naturally for 5 minutes, then do a quick pressure release.
3. For the yogurt sauce, combine yogurt, garlic, salt, fresh dill, and lemon juice.

## Nutrition

- Calories: 388
- Fat: 32.4 g.
- Net carbs: 7.9 g.
- Protein: 13.5 g.

# 89. Shrimp With Linguine

**Preparation time:** 10 minutes

**Cooking time:** 10 minutes

**Servings:** 4

## Ingredients

- 1 tbsp. butter
- 1 lb. linguine
- 1 lb. shrimp, cleaned
- ½ c. white wine
- 2 garlic cloves, minced
- ½ c. Parmesan cheese, shredded
- 2 c. parsley, chopped
- Salt and pepper, to taste
- ½ c. coconut cream, for garnish
- ½ avocado, diced, for garnish
- 1 tbsp. fresh dill, for garnish

## Directions

1. Melt the butter on Sauté. Stir in the garlic clove, linguine, and parsley. Cook for 4 minutes until aromatic. Add white wine and shrimp; season with pepper and salt, seal the lid.

2. Choose "Manual" and cook for 5 minutes on high pressure. When completes, quickly release the pressure. Unseal and remove the lid.
3. Press Sauté, put the cheese, and stir well until combined, for 30–40 seconds. Serve topped with avocado, dill, and coconut cream.

## Nutrition

- Calories: 412
- Net carbs: 5.6
- Fat: 21 g.
- Protein: 48 g.

# 90. Mexican Cod Fillets

**Preparation time:** 10 minutes

**Cooking time:** 10 minutes

**Servings:** 3

## Ingredients

- 1 onion, sliced
- 3 cod fillets
- 2 c. cabbage
- 1 Jalapeno pepper
- Juice from 1 lemon
- ½ tsp. oregano
- ½ tsp. cayenne pepper
- ½ tsp. cumin powder
- 1 tbsp. olive oil
- Salt and black pepper to taste

## Directions

1. Heat the oil on Sauté, and add cabbage, onion, jalapeño pepper, lemon juice, cumin powder, cayenne pepper, and oregano, and stir to combine. Cook for about 8–10 minutes.
2. Season with black pepper and salt. Arrange the cod fillets in the sauce, using a spoon to cover each piece with some of the sauce.
3. Seal the lid and select Manual. Cook for 5 minutes on High pressure. When completed, do a quick release and serve.

## Nutrition

- Calories: 306
- Net carbs: 6.8 g.
- Fat: 19.4 g.
- Protein: 21 g.

# 91. Simple Mushroom Chicken Mix

**Preparation time:** 5 minutes

**Cooking time:** 18 minutes

**Servings:** 2

## Ingredients

- ½ lb. chicken, cooked and mashed
- 2 tomatoes, chopped
- 1 tbsp. butter
- 1 c. broccoli, chopped
- 2 tbsps. mayonnaise
- 1 onion, sliced
- Salt and pepper, to taste
- ½ c. mushroom soup

## Directions

1. Put the cooked chicken into a bowl. In a separate bowl, mix the mayo, tomatoes, broccoli mushroom soup, onion, pepper, and salt. Add the chicken.
2. Grease a round baking tray with butter. Place the mixture in a tray. Put 2 c. water into the Instant Pot and place the trivet inside.
3. Place the tray on top. Seal the lid, select "Manual," and cook for 14 minutes on high pressure. When ready, do a quick release.

## Nutrition

- Calories: 561
- Net carbs: 6.3 g.
- Fat: 49.5 g.
- Protein: 28.5 g.

## 92. Squash Spaghetti With Bolognese Sauce

**Preparation time:** 5 minutes

**Cooking time:** 10 minutes

**Servings:** 3

### Ingredients

- 2 c. water
- Bolognese sauce to serve
- 1 large squash, cut into 2 and seed pulp removed

### Directions

1. Put the trivet and add water. Add in the squash, seal the lid, choose Manual and cook on high pressure for 8 minutes.
2. Once completed, quickly release the pressure. Remove the squash; use two forks to shred the inner skin. Serve with Bolognese sauce.

### Nutrition

- Calories: 37
- Net carbs: 7.8 g.
- Fat: 0.4 g.
- Protein: 0.9 g.

## 93. **Healthy Halibut Fillets**

**Preparation time:** 5 minutes

**Cooking time:** 10 minutes

**Servings:** 2

### Ingredients

- 1 tbsp. dill
- 2 halibut fillets
- tbsp onion powder
- c. parsley, chopped
- tbsp. paprika
- tbsp. garlic powder
- tbsp. lemon pepper
- tbsp. lemon juice

### Directions

1. Mix lemon pepper, lemon juice, garlic powder, parsley, onion powder, paprika, dill in a bowl. Pour the mixture into the Instant pot and put the halibut fish over it.
2. Seal the lid, press "Manual" mode, and cook for 10 minutes on high pressure. When completed, do a quick pressure release by setting the valve to venting.

### Nutrition

- Calories: 283
- Net carbs: 6.2 g.
- Fat: 16.4 g.
- Protein: 22.5 g.

# 94. Clean Salmon With Soy Sauce

**Preparation time:** 10 minutes

**Cooking time:** 30 minutes

**Servings:** 2

## Ingredients

- 2 tbsps. avocado oil
- 2 salmon fillets
- 1 tbsp. garlic powder
- 2 tbsps. soy sauce
- 2 tbsps. fresh dill to garnish
- Salt and pepper, to taste

## Directions

1. For the marinade, mix the avocado oil, soy sauce, pepper, salt, and garlic powder into a bowl. Dip salmon in the mixture and put in the refrigerator for 20 minutes.
2. Transfer to the Instant pot. Seal, set on "Manual," and cook for 10 minutes on high pressure.
3. When completed, do a quick release. Serve topped with the fresh dill.

## Nutrition

- Calories: 512
- Fat: 21 g.
- Net carbs: 3.2 g.
- Protein: 65 g.

## 95. Simple Salmon With Eggs

**Preparation time:** 2 minutes

**Cooking time:** 5 minutes

**Servings:** 3

### Ingredients

- 2 eggs, whisked
- 1 lb. salmon, cooked, mashed
- 2 onions, chopped
- 1 c. parsley, chopped
- 2 stalks celery, chopped
- 2 tbsps. olive oil
- Salt and pepper, to taste

### Directions

1. Mix onion, salmon, parsley, celery, and salt and pepper, in a bowl. Form into 6 patties about 1-inch thick and dip them in the whisked eggs. Heat oil in the Instant pot on Sauté mode.
2. Put the patties in the pot and cook on both sides, for about 5 minutes and transfer to the plate. Cool and serve.

### Nutrition

- Calories: 331
- Net carbs: 5.3 g.
- Fat: 16 g.
- Protein: 38 g.

## 96. Easy Shrimp

**Preparation time:** 4 minutes

**Cooking time:** 5 minutes

**Servings:** 2

### Ingredients

- 1 garlic cloves, crushed
- 1 lb. Shrimp, peeled and deveined
- 1 tbsp. butter
- A pinch of red pepper
- Salt and pepper, to taste
- 1 c. parsley, chopped

### Directions

1. Melt butter on "Sauté" mode. Add garlic, shrimp, red pepper, pepper, and salt.
2. Cook for about 5 minutes, stirring rarely the shrimp until pink. Serve with parsley.

### Nutrition

- Calories: 245
- Net carbs: 4.8 g.
- Fat: 4 g.
- Protein: 45 g.

# 97. Mushroom Pork Chops

**Preparation time:** 10 minutes

**Cooking time:** 40 minutes

**Servings:** 2

## Ingredients

- 8 oz. mushrooms, sliced
- 1 tsp. garlic
- 1 onion, peeled and chopped
- 1 c. intermittent-friendly mayonnaise
- 2 pork chops, boneless
- 1 tsp. ground nutmeg
- 1 tbsp. balsamic vinegar
- ½ c. coconut oil

## Directions

1. Get a pan and place it over medium heat. Put oil and let it heat up. Add onions, mushrooms, and stir. Cook for 4 minutes.
2. Add pork chops, season with garlic powder, nutmeg, and brown each side. Transfer the pan to the oven and bake for 30 minutes at 350°F. Place the pork chops on plates and keep them warm.
3. Take a pan and place it over medium heat. Add mayonnaise vinegar, over the mushroom mixture, and stir for a few minutes.
4. Put sauce over pork chops.

## Nutrition

- Calories: 600
- Net Carbohydrates: 5 g.
- Carbohydrates: 8 g.
- Protein: 30 g.
- Fat: 10 g.
- Fiber: 2 g.

# 98. Mediterranean Pork

**Preparation time:** 10 minutes

**Cooking time:** 35 minutes

**Servings:** 2

## Ingredients

- Salt and pepper, to taste
- 2 pork chops, bone-in
- 1 garlic clove, peeled and minced
- ½ tsp. dried rosemary

## Directions

1. Season pork chops with salt and pepper. Place in a roasting pan. Add rosemary, garlic to the pan.
2. Preheat the oven to 425°F. Bake for 10 minutes. Reduce heat to 350°F. Roast for 25 minutes more. Slice the pork and divide it among plates.
3. Drizzle pan juice all over. Serve and enjoy!

## Nutrition

- Calories: 165
- Fat: 2 g.
- Carbohydrates: 2 g.
- Protein: 26 g.
- Fiber: 1 g.
- Net carbs: 1 g.

## 99. Brie-Packed Smoked Salmon

**Preparation time:** 4 minutes

**Cooking time:** 0 minutes

**Servings:** 4

### Ingredients

- 4 oz. Brie round
- 1 tbsp. fresh dill
- 1 tbsp. lemon juice
- 2 oz. smoked salmon

### Directions

1. Cut Brie in half lengthwise.
2. Spread dill, salmon, and lemon juice over the Brie cheese.
3. Place the other half on top.
4. Serve with cauliflower bites/celery sticks.

### Nutrition

- Calories: 241
- Net carbs: 0 g.
- Fat: 19 g.
- Protein: 18 g.
- Carbohydrates: 3 g.
- Fiber: 2 g.

# 100.    Blackened Tilapia

**Preparation time:** 9 minutes

**Cooking time:** 9 minutes

**Servings:** 2

## Ingredients

- 1 tsp. red pepper flakes
- 1 c. cauliflower, chopped
- 1 tbsp. garlic, minced
- 1 tbsp. Italian seasoning
- 6 oz. tilapia
- 1 c. English cucumber, chopped with peel
- 1 tbsp. olive oil
- 1 sprig dill, chopped
- 1 tsp. Stevia
- 1 tbsp. lime juice
- 2 tbsps. Cajun blackened seasoning

## Directions

1. Take a bowl and put the seasoning ingredients (except Cajun). Add a tbsp. oil and whip. Pour dressing over cucumber and cauliflower. Brush the fish with olive oil on both sides.
2. Take a skillet and grease it well with 1 tbsp. olive oil. Press Cajun seasoning on both sides of the fish.
3. Cook fish for 3 minutes on each side. Serve with vegetables.

## Nutrition

- Calories: 530
- Net carbs: 4 g.
- Fat: 33 g.
- Carbohydrates: 2 g.
- Protein: 32 g.
- Fiber: 2 g.

# 101. Salsa Chicken Bites

**Preparation time:** 4 minutes

**Cooking time:** 14 minutes

**Servings:** 2

## Ingredients

- 1 c. salsa
- 2 chicken rest
- 2 taco seasoning mix
- 1 c. plain Greek yogurt
- ½ c. cheddar cheese, cubed

## Directions

1. Get a skillet and place it over medium heat.
2. Add a ½ c. salsa, chicken breast, and taco seasoning.
3. Combine well and cook for 12–15 minutes until the chicken is done.
4. Take the chicken out and cube them.
5. Put the cubes on a toothpick and top with cheddar.
6. Place yogurt and the remaining salsa in c. and use them as dips.
7. Serve.

## Nutrition

- Calories: 359
- Net carbs: 14 g.
- Fat: 14 g.
- Protein: 43 g.
- Fiber: 3 g.
- Carbohydrates: 17 g.

# 102.    Tomato & Tuna Balls

**Preparation time:** 25 minutes

**Cooking time:** 0

**Servings:** 2

## Ingredients

- 1 tbsp. capers
- 8 tomatoes, medium
- 3 oz. can of tuna, drained
- 10 Kalamata olives, pitted and minced
- 1 tbsp. parsley
- 2 tbsps. olive oil
- ½ tsp. thyme
- Salt, to taste
- Pepper, as needed

## Directions

1. Line a cookie pan with a paper towel and scoop guts out from the tomatoes.
2. Keep the tomato shells on the side.
3. Take a bowl and mix tuna, olives, capers, thyme, pepper, parsley, in a bowl and mix.
4. Put oil and mix. Fill the tomato shells with tuna mix.
5. Enjoy!

## Nutrition

- Calories: 169
- Net Carbohydrates: 5 g.
- Carbohydrates: 10 g.
- Fat: 10 g.
- Fiber: 5 g.
- Protein: 13 g.

## 103.    Spinach Almond Tortilla

**Preparation time:** 5 minutes

**Cooking time:** 10 minutes

**Servings:** 3

### Ingredients

- 1 c. almond flour + extra for dusting
- 1 c. spinach, chopped
- ¼ tbsp chili flakes
- ¼ c. mushrooms, sliced
- ½ tbsp. salt
- 2 tbsps. olive oil

### Directions

1. In a bowl, combine flour, spinach, salt, mushrooms, and flakes; mix well. Add ¼ c. water and make a thick batter.
2. Roll out the batter until is thin. Heat oil on Sauté mode.
3. Cook the tortilla until golden brown for 5 minutes. Serve with cilantro sauce and enjoy.

### Nutrition

- Calories: 165
- Net carbs: 2.1 g.
- Protein: 5 g.
- Fat: 9 g.

# 104.    Chicken and Peanut Stir-Fry

**Preparation time:** 5 minutes

**Cooking time:** 0

**Servings:** 2

## Ingredients

- 2 chicken thighs, cubed
- ½ c. broccoli florets
- ¼ c. peanuts
- 1 tbsp. sesame oil
- 1 ½ tbsp. soy sauce

## For the seasoning:

- ½ tsp. garlic powder

## Directions

1. Take a skillet pan, place it over medium heat, add ½ tbsp. oil and when hot, add chicken cubes and cook for 4 minutes until browned on all sides.
2. Then add broccoli florets and continue cooking for 2 minutes until tender-crisp.
3. Add the remaining ingredients, stir well and cook for another 2 minutes.
4. Serve.

## Nutrition 266

- Calories: 19 g.
- Fat: 18.5 g.
- Protein: 4 g.
- Net carbs: 2.5 g.
- Fiber: 1 g

# 105.     Chicken Scarpariello With Spicy Sausage

**Preparation time:** 10 minutes

**Cooking time:** 45 minutes

**Servings:** 6

## Ingredients

- 1 lb. boneless chicken thighs
- Sea salt, for seasoning
- Freshly ground black pepper, for seasoning
- 3 tbsps. good-quality olive oil, divided
- ½ lb. Italian sausage (sweet or hot)
- 1 tbsp. minced garlic
- 1 pimiento, chopped
- ¼ c. dry white wine
- 1 c. chicken stock
- 2 tbsps. chopped fresh parsley

## Directions

1. Preheat the oven. Set the oven temperature to 425°F.
2. Brown the sausage and chicken. Pat the chicken thighs to dry using paper towels and season them lightly with pepper and salt. In a large oven-safe skillet over medium-high heat, warm 2 tbsps. the olive oil. Put the chicken thighs and sausage to the skillet and brown them on all sides, turning them carefully, about 10 minutes.
3. Bake the sausage and chicken. Bring the skillet into the oven and bake for 25 minutes or until the chicken is cooked through. Take the skillet out of the oven, transfer the chicken and sausage to a plate, and put the skillet over medium heat on the stovetop.
4. Make the sauce. Heat the remaining 1 tbsp. olive oil, add the pimiento and garlic, and sauté for 3 minutes. Pour the white wine and deglaze the skillet by using a spoon to scrape up any browned bits from the bottom of the skillet. Pour in the chicken stock and bring it to a boil, then lessen the heat to low and simmer until the sauce reduces by about half, about 6 minutes.
5. Serve. Put back the sausage and chicken to the skillet, toss it to coat it with the sauce, and serve it topped with the parsley.

## Nutrition

- Calories: 370

- Total carbs: 3 g.
- Total fat: 30 g.
- Net carbs: 3 g.
- Fiber: 0 g.
- Protein: 19 g.
- Sodium: 314 mg.

# 106.    Almond Chicken Cutlets

**Preparation time:** 10 minutes

**Cooking time:** 15 minutes

**Servings:** 4

## Ingredients

- ½ tsp. garlic powder
- 2 eggs
- 1 c. almond flour
- 4 (4 oz.) boneless skinless chicken breasts, pounded to about ¼-inch thick
- 1 tbsp. chopped fresh oregano
- 2 tbsps. grass-fed butter
- ¼ c. good-quality olive oil

## Directions

1. Whisk together the garlic powder, eggs, in a medium bowl, and set it aside. Mix together the oregano and almond flour on a plate and set the plate next to the egg mixture. Pat the chicken breasts to dry using paper towels and dip them into the egg mixture. Remove excess egg then roll the chicken in the almond flour until they are coated.
2. In a huge skillet over medium-high heat, warm the olive oil and butter. Put the breaded chicken breasts and fry them, turning them once, until they are very crispy, cooked through, and golden brown, and 14–16 minutes.
3. Serve. Place one cutlet on each of the 4 plates and serve them immediately.

## Nutrition

- Calories: 328

- Total carbs: 0 g.
- Total fat: 23 g.
- Net carbs: 0 g.
- Fiber: 0 g.
- Protein: 28 g.
- Sodium: 75 mg.

# 107. Slow Cooker Chicken Cacciatore

**Preparation time:** 15 minutes

**Cooking time:** 10 minutes

**Servings:** 4

## Ingredients

- 4 (4 oz.) boneless chicken breasts, each cut into three pieces
- ¼ c. good-quality olive oil
- 1 onion, chopped
- 1 c. sliced mushrooms
- 2 celery stalks, chopped
- 2 tbsps. minced garlic
- 1 (28 oz.) can of sodium-free diced tomatoes
- ½ c. red wine
- 1 tbsp. dried basil
- ½ c. tomato paste
- ⅛ tsp. red pepper flakes
- 1 tsp. dried oregano

## Directions

1. Warm the olive oil in a skillet at medium-high heat. Add the chicken breasts and brown them, turning them once, about 10 minutes in total.
2. Cook in the slow cooker. Place the chicken in the slow cooker and stir in the onion, mushrooms, celery, garlic, red wine, tomatoes, tomato paste, basil, red pepper flakes, and oregano. Cook it on high for around 3–4 hours or on low for 6–8 hours, until the chicken is fully cooked and tender.
3. Serve. Split the chicken and sauce between four bowls and serve it immediately.

## Nutrition

- Calories: 383
- Total carbs: 11 g.
- Total fat: 26 g.
- Fiber: 4 g.
- Sodium: 116 mg.
- Net carbs: 7 g.
- Protein: 26 g.

# 108. Cheesy Chicken Sun-Dried Tomato Packets

**Preparation time:** 15 minutes

**Cooking time:** 40 minutes

**Servings:** 4

## Ingredients

- ½ c. chopped oil-packed sun-dried tomatoes
- 1 c. goat cheese
- 1 tsp. minced garlic
- ½ tsp. dried basil
- 4 (4 oz.) boneless chicken breasts
- ½ tsp. dried oregano
- Sea salt, for seasoning
- 3 tbsps. olive oil
- Freshly ground black pepper, for seasoning

## Directions

1. Heat the oven temperature to 375°F.
2. In a medium bowl, put the sun-dried tomatoes, goat cheese, garlic, oregano, and basil, then mix until everything is well blended.
3. Create a horizontal slice in the middle of each chicken breast to make a pocket, making sure not to cut through the sides or ends. Ladle one-quarter of the filling into each breast, folding the skin and chicken meat over the slit to form packets. Secure the packets with a toothpick. Lightly season the breasts with salt and pepper.
4. Warm the olive oil in a large oven-safe skillet over medium heat. Add the breasts and sear them, turning them once, until they are golden about 8 minutes in total.
5. Bring the skillet into the oven and bake the chicken for 30 minutes or until it's cooked through.
6. Remove the toothpicks. Split the chicken into 4 plates and serve them immediately.

## Nutrition

- Calories: 388
- Total carbs: 4 g.
- Total fat: 29 g.
- Fiber: 1 g.
- Sodium: 210 mg.
- Net carbs: 3 g.

- Protein: 28 g.

# 109. Tuscan Chicken Sauté

**Preparation time:** 10 minutes

**Cooking time:** 35 minutes

**Servings:** 4

## Ingredients

- Sea salt, for seasoning
- 1 lb. boneless chicken breasts, each cut into three pieces
- Freshly ground black pepper, for seasoning
- 1 tbsp. minced garlic
- 3 tbsps. olive oil
- ¾ c. chicken stock
- ½ tsp. dried basil
- 1 tsp. dried oregano
- ½ c. heavy, whipping, cream
- 1 c. fresh spinach
- ¼ c. sliced Kalamata olives
- ½ c. shredded Asiago cheese

## Directions

1. Pat, the chicken, breasts dry and season them with salt and pepper.
2. Warm the olive oil in a huge skillet over medium-high heat. Add the chicken and sauté until it is golden brown and just cooked through, about 15 minutes in total. Transfer the chicken to a plate and set it aside.
3. Put the garlic to the skillet, then sauté until it's softened for about 2 minutes. Stir in the oregano, chicken stock, and basil, scraping up any browned bits in the skillet. Bring to a boil, then reduce the heat to low and simmer until the sauce is reduced by about one-quarter, about 10 minutes.
4. Stir in the Asiago, cream, and simmer, stirring the sauce frequently, until it has thickened about 5 minutes. Put back the chicken to the skillet along with any accumulated juices. Stir in the olives and spinach and simmer until the spinach is wilted for about 2 minutes.
5. Divide the chicken and sauce between 4 plates and serve it immediately.

## Nutrition

- Calories: 483
- Total carbs: 5 g.
- Total fat: 38 g.
- Net carbs: 3 g.
- Protein: 31 g.
- Fiber: 1 g.
- Sodium: 332 mg.

# 110.    Easy Chicken Tacos

**Preparation time:** 5 minutes

**Cooking time:** 27 minutes

**Servings:** 4

## Ingredients

- 1 lb. ground chicken
- 1 ½ c. Mexican cheese blend
- 1 tbsp. Mexican seasoning blend
- 2 tsps. butter, room temperature
- 2 small-sized shallots, peeled and finely chopped
- 1 garlic clove, minced
- 1 c. tomato puree
- ½ c. salsa
- 2 slices bacon, chopped

## Directions

1. Put butter then melt in over a moderately high flame in a saucepan. Cook the shallots until tender and fragrant.
2. Then, sauté the chicken, garlic, and bacon for about 5 minutes, stirring continuously and crumbling with a fork. Put them in a Mexican seasoning blend.
3. Fold in the salsa and tomato puree; continue to boil for 5–7 minutes over medium-low heat; reserve.
4. Line a baking pan with wax paper. Put 4 piles of the shredded cheese on the baking pan and gently press them down with a wide spatula to make "taco shells."
5. Bake in the oven at 365°F. for 6–7 minutes or until melted. Cool for about 10 minutes.

## Nutrition

- Calories: 535
- Carbs: 4.8 g.
- Fat: 33.3 g.
- Fiber: 1.9 g.
- Protein: 47.9 g.

## 111.  Cheesy Bacon-Wrapped Chicken With Asparagus Spears

**Preparation time:** 20 minutes

**Cooking time:** 30 minutes

**Servings:** 4

### Ingredients

- 8 bacon slices
- 4 chicken breasts
- 1 lb. (454 g.) asparagus spears
- ½ c. Manchego cheese, grated
- 2 tbsps. fresh lemon juice
- Salt, to taste
- Freshly ground black pepper, to taste
- 4 tbsps. olive oil, divided

### Directions

1. Put the oven to 400°F. Line a baking sheet using parchment paper, then grease with 1 tbsp. olive oil.
2. Put the chicken breasts in a huge bowl, and drizzle with salt and black pepper. Toss to combine well.
3. Wrap every chicken breast with 2 slices of bacon. Put the chicken on the baking sheet, then bake in the preheated oven for 25 minutes or until the bacon is crispy.
4. Preheat the grill to high, then brush with the remaining olive oil.
5. Put the asparagus spears on the grill grate, and sprinkle with salt. Grill for 5 minutes or until fork-tender. Flip the asparagus regularly during the grilling.
6. Place the bacon-wrapped chicken breasts on four plates, drizzle with lemon juice, and scatter with Manchego cheese. Spread the hot asparagus spears on top to serve.

### Nutrition

- Calories: 455
- Net carbs: 2 g.
- Protein: 26.1 g.
- Total fat: 38.1 g.

# 112.    Zucchini Noodles in Garlic and Parmesan Toss

**Preparation time:** 5 minutes

**Cooking time:** 15 minutes

**Servings:** 4

## Ingredients

- 3 large zucchinis, spiralized
- 2 tbsps. olive oil
- 3 garlic cloves, minced
- 1 lemon, zested and juiced
- Salt to taste
- Black pepper to taste
- 5 mint leaves, chopped
- 6 tbsps. Parmesan cheese, grated

## Directions

1. Set on Sauté. Heat the oil, and add garlic, salt, and lemon zest. Stir and cook for 30 seconds. Put the zucchini and pour lemon juice over.
2. Coat the noodles fast but gently with the oil.
3. Cook for 10 seconds, press "Cancel." Sprinkle the cheese and mint leaves over and toss gently.

## Nutrition

- Calories: 15
- Fat: 2 g.
- Protein: 10 g.
- Net carbs: 2 g.

# 113.    Lemonade Broccoli

**Preparation time:** 5 minutes

**Cooking time:** 10 minutes

**Servings:** 3

## Ingredients

- 1 lb. broccoli, cut in bite sizes
- 3 lemon slices
- ¼ c. water
- Salt to taste
- Pepper to taste

## Directions

1. Pour the water into the Instant Pot. Put the broccoli and sprinkle with pepper, lemon juice, and salt. Seal the lid, secure the pressure valve, and "Manual" in low-pressure mode for 3 minutes.
2. Once completed, quickly release the pressure.
3. Drain the broccoli and serve as a side dish.

## Nutrition

- Calories: 34
- Fat: 0.4 g.
- Net carbs: 5.6 g.
- Protein: 2.8 g.

# 114.    Beets With Yogurt

**Preparation time:** 10 minutes

**Cooking time:** 40 minutes

**Servings:** 3–4

## Ingredients

- 1 lime, zested and juiced
- 1 lb. beets, washed
- 1 garlic clove, minced
- 1 c. plain full milk yogurt
- Salt to taste
- 1 c. water
- 1 tbsp. olive oil to drizzle
- 1 tbsp. fresh dill, chopped
- Black pepper to garnish

## Directions

1. Pour the water into the Instant Pot and fit in a steamer basket.
2. Put the beets, seal the lid, secure the pressure valve, and select "Manual" mode on high-pressure mode for 30 minutes.
3. Once completed, do a natural pressure release for 10 minutes, then quickly release the remaining pressure.
4. Remove the beets to a bowl to cool, and then remove the skin. Slice into wedges.
5. Place beets in a dip plate, drizzle the olive oil and lime juice over; set aside.
6. Mix yogurt garlic, and lime zest in a bowl.
7. Pour over the beets and garnish with salt, black pepper, and dill.

## Nutrition

- Calories: 102
- Net carbs: 8.2 g.
- Fat: 3.8 g.
- Protein: 5.7 g.

# 115.   Vegetarian Faux Stew

**Preparation time:** 5 minutes

**Cooking time:** 25 minutes

**Servings:** 3

## Ingredients

- ½ c. diced tomatoes
- 4 cloves garlic
- 1 tsp. minced ginger
- 1 tsp. turmeric
- 1 tsp. cayenne powder
- 2 tsps. paprika
- Salt to taste
- 1 tsp. cumin powder
- 2 c. dry soy curls
- 1 ½ c. water
- 3 tbsps. butter
- ½ c. heavy cream
- ¼ c. chopped cilantro

## Directions

1. Place the tomatoes, soy curls, water, and all spices in the Instant Pot. Cover the lid, secure the pressure valve and select Manual mode on High-Pressure mode for 6 minutes.
2. Once completed, do a natural pressure release for 10 minutes. Select Sauté, add the butter and cream. Stir while crushing the tomatoes with the back of the spoon. Stir in the cilantro and serve.

## Nutrition

- Calories: 143
- Net carbs: 2 g.
- Fat: 9 g.
- Protein: 4 g.

# 116.    Vegetable en Papillote

**Preparation time:** 5 minutes

**Cooking time:** 15 minutes

**Servings:** 3

## Ingredients

- 4 small carrots, widely julienned
- 1 c. green beans
- ¼ tsp. black pepper
- 1 garlic clove, crushed
- A pinches salt
- 2 tbsps. butter
- 1 tbsp. chopped thyme
- 2 slices lemon
- 1 tbsp. oregano
- 17-inch parchment paper
- 1 tbsp. chopped parsley

## Directions

1. Add all ingredients, except butter and lemon slices in a bowl and toss. Place the paper on a flat surface and add the mixed ingredients in the middle of the paper. Put the lemon slices on top and drop the butter over. Wrap it up well.
2. Add 1 c. water in and lower the trivet with the handle.
3. Put the veggie pack on the trivet, cover the lid, and cook under high pressure for 2 minutes. Once completed, do a quick release. Carefully remove the packet and serve veggies in a wrap on a plate.

## Nutrition

- Calories: 60
- Net carbs: 1 g.
- Fat: 3 g.
- Protein: 3 g.

# 117. Faux Beet Risotto

**Preparation time:** 5 minutes

**Cooking time:** 15 minutes

**Servings:** 2

## Ingredients

- 2 tbsps. olive oil
- 4 beets, tails and leaves removed
- 1 big head cauliflower, cut into florets
- 4 tbsps. full milk
- 2 tsps. red chili flakes
- Salt to taste
- Black pepper to taste
- ½ c. water

## Directions

1. Pour the water into the Instant Pot and fit a steamer basket. Place the cauliflower and beets in the basket. Cover the lid, and cook on High-Pressure mode for 4 minutes.
2. Once completed, do a natural pressure release for 10 minutes, then quickly release the pressure. Remove the steamer basket with the vegetables and throw away water. Remove the beets' peels.
3. Place veggies back in the pot, add pepper, salt, and flakes. Mash with a potato masher. Hit Sauté, and cook the milk for 2 minutes. Stir regularly. Dish onto plates and drizzle with oil.

## Nutrition

- Calories: 153
- Net carbs: 2.5 g.
- Fat: 9 g.
- Protein: 3.6 g.

# 118.  Broccoli Rice With Mushrooms

**Preparation time:** 5 minutes

**Cooking time:** 30 minutes

**Servings:** 3

## Ingredients

- 1 tbsp. olive oil
- 1 small red onion, chopped
- 1 carrot, chopped
- 2 c. button mushrooms, chopped
- ½ lemon, zested and juiced
- Salt to taste
- Pepper to taste
- 2 cloves garlic, minced
- ½ c. broccoli rice
- ½ c. chicken stock
- 5 cherry tomatoes
- Parsley leaves, chopped for garnishing

## Directions

1. Set on Sauté. Heat oil, and cook the onions and carrots for 2 minutes. Stir in mushrooms, and cook for 3 minutes. Stir in salt, pepper, garlic, lemon juice, and lemon zest.
2. Stir in chicken stock and broccoli. Drop the tomatoes over the top, but don't stir. Cover the lid, and cook on high pressure for 10 minutes. Once completed, do a natural pressure release for 4 minutes, then quickly release the remaining pressure. Dust with parsley and stir evenly.

## Nutrition

- Calories: 160
- Net carbs: 10 g.
- Fat: 2 g.
- Protein: 6 g.

# 119. Cucumber Avocado Salad With Bacon

**Preparation time:** 10 minutes

**Cooking time:** 0

**Servings:** 2

## Ingredients

- 1 c. fresh baby spinach, chopped
- ½ English cucumber, sliced thin
- 1 small avocado, pitted and chopped
- 1 ½ tbsp. olive oil
- 1 ½ tbsp. lemon juice
- Salt and pepper
- 2 slices cooked bacon, chopped

## Directions

1. Combine the cucumber, spinach, and avocado in a salad bowl.
2. Toss with lemon juice, olive oil, salt, and pepper.
3. Top with sliced bacon to serve.

## Nutrition

- Calories: 365
- Protein: 7 g.
- Fat: 24.5 g.
- Carbs: 13 g.
- Net carbs: 5 g.
- Fiber: 8 g.

# 120.    Baked Cod With Cucumber-Dill Salsa

**Preparation time:** 20 minutes

**Cooking time:** 10 minutes

**Servings:** 3

## Ingredients

### For the cucumber salsa:

- 2 tsps. fresh dill juice of 1 lime zest of 1 lime
- ¼ c. boiling red pepper ½ tsp. of granulated sugar
- ½ English cucumber, diced

### For the fish:

- Juice of 1 lemon
- 12 oz. cod fillets, deboned and divided into 3 parts
- 1 tbsp. olive oil
- ½ tbsps. freshly ground black pepper

## Directions

1. Combine the cucumber together in a small bowl.
2. Preheat the oven to 360°F. Put the fish on a pie plate and squeeze the juice over the fillets evenly.
3. Dust over the fillets evenly with pepper and drizzle the olive oil. Bake the fish with a fork for about 6 minutes or until it easily flakes.
4. Transfer the fish to 3 plates and serve on top with the salsa of cucumber.

## Nutrition

- Carbohydrates: 3 g.
- Phosphorus: 120 mg.
- Fat: 2 g.
- Potassium: 286 mg.
- Protein: 20 mg.
- Sodium: 68 mg.

## 121.    **Roasted Whole Chicken**

**Preparation time:** 20 minutes

**Cooking time:** 1 hour and 32 minutes

**Servings:** 6

### Ingredients

- 3 garlic cloves, minced
- 2 tbsps. unsalted butter
- Salt and ground black pepper, as required
- 1 (3 lbs.) grass-fed whole chicken, neck, and giblets removed

### Directions

1. Preheat the oven to 400°F. Organize the oven rack into the lower portion of the oven.
2. Grease a huge baking dish.
3. Put the butter and garlic in a small pan over medium heat and cook for about 1–2 minutes.
4. Remove the pan from heat and let it cool for about 2 minutes.
5. Season the outside and inside of the chicken evenly with salt and black pepper.
6. Arrange the chicken into a prepared baking dish, breast side up.
7. Dispense the garlic butter over and inside of the chicken.
8. Bake for about 1–1 ½ hours, basting with the pan juices every 20 minutes.
9. Remove from the oven and place the chicken onto a cutting board for about 5–10 minutes before carving.
10. Slice into desired size pieces and serve.

### Nutrition

- Calories: 772
- Protein: 99 g.
- Net carbs: 0.7 g.
- Fat: 39.1 g.

# 122. Buffalo Pizza Chicken

**Preparation time:** 5 minutes

**Cooking time:** 5–6 minutes

**Servings:** 5

## Ingredients

- ½ c. buffalo-style hot sauce
- Vegetable cooking spray
- 1 (16 oz.) package prebaked Italian pizza crust
- 1 c. (4 oz.) shredded Provolone cheese
- ¼ c. crumbled blue cheese
- 2 c. chopped deli-roasted whole chicken

## Directions

1. Coat the grill with the spray and set it on the grill. Preheat grill to 350°F (medium heat).
2. Spread the hot sauce over the crust, and the succeeding 3 ingredients surface.
3. Put the crust on the cooking grate directly. Grill at 350°F (medium heat) for 4 min, covered with the grill lid.
4. Rotate 1-quarter turn pizza and grill, covered with grill top, for 5–6 min or until heated thoroughly. Serve right away.

## Nutrition

- Calories: 365
- Net carbs: 42 g.
- Protein: 24 g.
- Fat: 11 g.

# 123. Hot Chicken Meatballs

**Preparation time:** 5 minutes

**Cooking time:** 21 minutes

**Servings:** 2

## Ingredients

- Salt and black pepper, to taste
- 1 lb. ground chicken
- ½ c. almond flour
- 2 tbsps. yellow mustard
- ¼ c. hot sauce
- 1 egg
- ¼ c. Mozzarella cheese, grated

## Directions

1. Preheat the oven to 400°F and line a baking tray with parchment paper.
2. Combine the chicken, mustard, black pepper, Mozzarella cheese, flour, egg, and salt in a bowl. Form meatballs and arrange them on the baking tray.
3. Cook for 16 minutes, then dispense over the hot sauce and bake for 5 more minutes.

## Nutrition

- Calories: 487
- Protein: 31.5 g.
- Net carbs: 4.3 g.
- Fat: 35 g.

# 124. Intermittent Chicken Enchiladas

**Preparation time:** 10 minutes

**Cooking time:** 25 minutes

**Servings:** 6

## Ingredients

- 2 c. gluten-free enchilada sauce

  Chicken:
- 1 tbsp. avocado oil
- 4 cloves garlic, minced

- 3 c. shredded chicken, cooked
- ¼ c. chicken broth
- ¼ c. fresh cilantro, chopped

Assembly:
- 6 Coconut tortillas
- ¾ c. Colby jack cheese, shredded
- ¼ c. green onions, chopped

## Direction

1. Put oil at medium to high heat in a large pan. Add the sliced garlic and cook until fragrant for about a minute.
2. Add 1 c. enchilada sauce (half the total), rice, coriander, and chicken. Boil for 5 minutes.
3. In the meantime, heat the oven to 375°F. Grease a 9x13-inch baking dish.
4. Place ¼ c. chicken mixture in the middle of each tortilla. Roll up and place seam side down in the baking dish.
5. Dispense the remaining c. enchilada sauce over the enchiladas. Sprinkle with shredded cheese.
6. Bake for 10–12 minutes. Sprinkle with green onions.

## Nutrition

- Calories: 349
- Protein: 31 g.
- Net carbs: 9 g.
- Fat: 19 g.

# 125.    Indian Chicken Curry

**Preparation time:** 20 minutes

**Cooking time:** 40 minutes

**Servings:** 6

## Ingredients

- 6 boneless, skinless chicken thighs
- 3 tbsps. of olive oil, divided
- 2 tbsps. of fresh garlic
- 1 small sweet onion
- 1 tbsp. of fresh ginger
- ¼ c. coconut milk
- ¾ c. water
- 1 tbsp. of hot curry powder
- 2 tbsps. of fresh cilantro.

## Directions

1. Place 2 tbsps. oil over medium to a high place in a huge skillet.
2. Put the chicken and roast for about 10 minutes until the thighs are browned over.
3. Remove the chicken on a plate with tongs and set aside.
4. In the skillet, add the remaining 1 tbsp. oil and sauté the garlic, onion, and ginger for about 3 minutes or until softened.
5. Remove the water, curry powder, and milk from the coconut.
6. Go back to the skillet with the chicken and bring the liquid to a boil.
7. Reduce heat to low, cover the skillet and cook for 26 minutes or until the chicken is tender and the sauce is thick. Serve with cilantro on hand.

## Nutrition

- Fat: 13 g.
- Phosphorus: 136 mg.
- Potassium: 230 mg.
- Carbohydrate: 2 g.
- Protein: 26 g.
- Sodium: 86 mg.

# 126.    Persian Chicken

**Preparation time:** 10 minutes

**Cooking time:** 20 minutes

**Servings:** 6

## Ingredients

- ¼ c. freshly squeezed lemon juice
- ½ small sweet onion
- ½ tbsp. sweet paprika
- 1 tbsp. dried oregano
- ½ tbsps. ground cumin
- 6 boneless, skinless chicken thighs
- ½ c. olive oil

## Directions

1. Insert the vegetables into a blender. Mix it well.
2. Place the olive while the motor is running.
3. In a sealable bag for the freezer, place the chicken thighs and put the mixture in the sealable bag.
4. Refrigerate it for 2 hours, while turning it 2 times.
5. Remove the marinade thighs and discard the additional marinade. Preheat to medium the barbecue. Grill the chicken, turning once or until the internal.

## Nutrition

- Fat: 21 g.
- Potassium: 220 mg.
- Carbohydrates: 3 g.
- Protein: 22 g.
- Sodium: 86 mg.

# 127.    **Pesto Pork Chops**

**Preparation time:** 20 minutes

**Cooking time:** 20 minutes

**Servings:** 3

## Ingredients

- 8 tbsps. herb pesto
- 3 (3 oz.) top-flood pork chops, boneless, fat
- 1 tbsp. olive oil
- ½ c. bread crumbs

## Directions

1. Preheat the oven to 360°F. Cover a foil baker's sheet; set aside.
2. Rub 1 tbsp. pesto evenly across each pork chop on both sides.
3. Every pork chop in the crumbs of bread is lightly dredged.
4. Heat the oil in a medium-high heat large skillet. Brown the pork chops for about 6 minutes on each side.
5. Place on the baking sheet the pork chops. Bake until the pork reaches 13°F in the middle for about 10 minutes.

## Nutrition

- Fat: 8 g.
- Phosphorus: 188 mg.
- Carbohydrates: 10 g.
- Sodium: 138 mg.
- Potassium: 220 mg.
- Protein: 23 g.

# 128. Roasted Red Pepper and Eggplant Soup

**Preparation time:** 20 minutes

**Cooking time:** 40 minutes

**Servings:** 6

## Ingredients

- 2 small red peppers, halved
- 1 small sweet onion, cut into quarters
- 2 c. eggplant
- 1 c. olive oil
- 2 garlic cloves, crushed
- 1 c. easy chicken stock
- ¼ c. chopped fresh basil
- Water

## Directions

1. Preheat the oven to 360°F. In a huge ovenproof baking dish, place the red peppers, onions, eggplant, and garlic.
2. Put the olive oil on the vegetables.
3. For about 40 minutes or until slightly charred and soft, roast the vegetables.
4. Slightly cool the vegetables and take the peppers away from the skin.
5. In a food processor (or in a huge bowl, using a handheld immersion blender) purée the vegetables with the chicken stock.
6. Move the soup to a large pot and add sufficient water to achieve the desired thickness. Heat the soup and put the basil to a simmer. Season with pepper and serve.

## Nutrition

- Carbohydrates: 8 g.
- Fat: 2 g.
- Potassium: 188 mg.
- Phosphorus: 33 mg.
- Protein: 2 g.
- Sodium: 86 mg.

## 129.　Fennel and Figs Lamb

**Preparation time:** 10 minutes

**Cooking time:** 40 minutes

**Servings:** 2

### Ingredients

- 6 oz. lamb racks
- 2 fennel bulbs, sliced
- Salt to taste
- Pepper, to taste
- 1 tbsp. olive oil
- 2 figs, cut in half
- ⅛ c. apple cider vinegar
- ½ tbsp. swerve

### Directions

1. Get a bowl and add figs, fennel, vinegar, oil swerve, and toss. Transfer to baking dish. Season with pepper and salt.
2. Bake it for 15 minutes at 400°F.
3. Season lamb with pepper, salt, and transfer to a heated pan over medium-high heat. Cook for a few minutes. Add lamb to the baking dish with fennel and bake for 20 minutes. Divide between plates and serve.

### Nutrition

- Fat: 3 g.
- Calories: 230
- Carbohydrates: 5 g.
- Protein: 10 g.
- Fiber: 2 g.
- Net carbs: 3 g.

# 130. Tamari Steak Salad

**Preparation time:** 15 minutes

**Cooking time:** 10 minutes

**Servings:** 2

## Ingredients

- 1 large bunches salad greens
- 4 oz. beefsteak
- ½ red bell pepper, diced
- 4 cherry tomatoes, cut into halves
- 1 radish, sliced
- 1 tbsp. olive oil
- ¼ tbsp. fresh lemon juice
- 1 oz. gluten-free tamari sauce
- Salt as needed

## Directions

1. Marinate steak in tamari sauce.
2. Make the salad by adding bell pepper, tomatoes, radish, salad green, oil, salt, and lemon juice to a bowl and toss them well.
3. Grill the steak to your wanted doneness and transfer steak on top of the salad platter.
4. Let it sit for 1 minute and chop it crosswise. Serve.

## Nutrition

- Calories: 500
- Carbohydrates: 4 g.
- Fat: 37 g.
- Protein: 33 g.
- Net Carbohydrates: 2 g.
- Fiber: 2 g.

## 131.    Blackened Chicken

**Preparation time:** 10 minutes

**Cooking time:** 10 minutes

**Servings:** 2

### Ingredients

- ⅛ tsp. salt
- ¼ tsp. paprika
- ¼ tsp. cayenne pepper
- ¼ tsp. dried thyme
- 1 chicken breast, boneless and skinless
- ¼ tsp. ground cumin
- ⅛ tsp. onion powder
- ⅛ tsp. ground white pepper

### Directions

1. Preheat the oven to 350°F. Grease baking sheet. Take a cast-iron skillet and place it over high heat.
2. Add oil and heat it for 5 minutes until smoking hot.
3. Take a small bowl and mix paprika, salt, cumin, cayenne, thyme, white pepper, onion powder. Oil the chicken breast on both sides and coat the breast with the spice mix.
4. Transfer to your hot pan and cook for 1 minute per side.
5. Transfer to your arranged baking sheet and bake for 5 minutes.
6. Serve and enjoy!

### Nutrition

- Calories: 136
- Carbohydrates: 2 g.
- Fat: 3 g.
- Net carbs: 1 g.
- Fiber: 1 g.
- Protein: 24 g.

# 132.    Mediterranean Mushroom Olive Steak

**Preparation time:** 10 minutes

**Cooking time:** 14 minutes

**Servings:** 2

## Ingredients

- ½ lb. boneless beef sirloin steak, ¾-inch thick, cut into 4 pieces
- ½ large red onion, chopped
- ½ c. mushrooms
- 2 garlic cloves, thinly sliced
- 2 tbsps. olive oil
- ¼ c. green olives, coarsely chopped
- ½ c. parsley leaves, finely cut

## Directions

1. Take a huge-sized skillet and place it over medium-high heat.
2. Add oil and let it heat up. Add beef and cook until both sides are browned, remove beef and drain fats. Add the rest of the oil to the skillet and heat it.
3. Add garlic, onions, and cook for 2–3 minutes. Stir well.
4. Add mushrooms olives and cook until mushrooms are thoroughly done. Return beef to skillet and lower heat to medium.
5. Cook for 3–4 minutes (covered). Stir in parsley. Serve!

## Nutrition

- Calories: 386
- Carbohydrates: 11 g.
- Fat: 30 g.
- Protein: 21 g.
- Net carbs: 6 g.
- Fiber: 5 g.

## 133.     Buttery Scallops

**Preparation time:** 10 minutes

**Cooking time:** 10 minutes

**Servings:** 6

### Ingredients

- 3 tbsps. butter, melted
- 2 lbs. sea scallops
- Salt and pepper, to taste
- 2 tbsps. fresh thyme, minced

### Directions

1. Preheat your air fryer to 390°F. Grease the air fryer cooking basket with butter.
2. Take a bowl, add all of the remaining ingredients, and toss well to coat the scallops.
3. Transfer scallops to air fryer-cooking basket and cook for 5 minutes.
4. Repeat if any ingredients are left, serve, and enjoy!

### Nutrition

- Calories: 186
- Total carbs: 4 g.
- Total fat: 24 g.
- Fiber: 1 g.
- Protein: 20 g.
- Net carbs: 2 g.

# 134.    Brussels Sprouts and Garlic Aioli

**Preparation time:** 15 minutes

**Cooking time:** 10 minutes

**Servings:** 4

## Ingredients

- 1 lb. Brussels sprouts, trimmed and excess leaves removed
- Salt and pepper, to taste
- 1 ½ tbsps. olive oil
- 2 tsps. lemon juice
- 1 tsp. powdered chili
- 2 garlic cloves
- ¾ c. whole egg, intermittent-friendly mayonnaise
- 3 c. water

## Directions

1. Take a skillet and place it over medium heat.
2. Add garlic cloves (with peel) and roast until fragrant and brown.
3. Remove skillet with garlic and put a pot with water over medium heat, bring the water to a boil.
4. Take a knife and cut Brussels sprouts in halves lengthwise, add them to the boiling water, blanch for 3 minutes.
5. Drain them through a sieve and keep them on the side.
6. Preheat your air fryer to 350°F.
7. Remove garlic from skillet and peel, crush them, and keep them on the side.
8. Add olive oil to skillet and place it over medium heat, stir in Brussels and season with pepper and salt and cook for 2 minutes.
9. Remove heat and transfer sprouts to your air fryer cooking basket, cook for 5 minutes. Make aioli by taking a small bowl and add crushed garlic, mayonnaise, lemon juice, powdered chili, salt, pepper, and mix.
10. Serve Brussels with the aioli, enjoy!

## Nutrition

- Calories: 42
- Total carbs: 3 g.
- Total fat: 2 g.

- Fiber: 1 g.
- Protein: 5 g.
- Net carbs: 2 g.

## 135.  Broccoli Bites

**Preparation time:** 15 minutes

**Cooking time:** 12 minutes

**Servings:** 4

### Ingredients

- ¼ c. Parmesan cheese, grated
- 2 eggs, beaten
- 2 c. broccoli florets
- Salt and pepper, to taste
- 1 ½ c. cheddar cheese, grated

### Directions

1. Add broccoli to the food processor and pulse until crumbly.
2. Mix broccoli and the remaining ingredients in a huge bowl.
3. Make small balls from the mixture and assemble them on a baking sheet.
4. Let it refrigerate for 30 minutes.
5. Preheat your Air Fryer to 360°F.
6. Transfer balls to air fryer cooking basket and cook for 12 minutes.
7. Serve.

### Nutrition

- Calories: 234
- Total carbs: 4 g.
- Total fat: 17 g.
- Fiber: 1 g.
- Protein: 16 g.

# Dessert

**136.**   **Strawberry Rhubarb Custard**

**Preparation time:** 4 hours and 5 minutes

**Cooking time:** 5 minutes

**Servings:** 5

## Ingredients

- 27 oz. coconut milk, full-fat
- 2 eggs
- ¾ c. strawberries, fresh
- ½ c. rhubarb, chopped
- ¼ c collagen, grass-fed
- 1 tsp vanilla extract, unsweetened
- 1/16 tsp. Stevia, liquid
- 1/16 tsp. salt
- 1 ½ tbsps. gelatin, grass-fed
- 1 c. water

## Directions

1. Place all the ingredients in a food processor except for the gelatin and water, pulse until smooth, then add gelatin and blend until smooth.
2. Divide the custard evenly between five half-pint jars and cover with their lid.
3. Switch on the instant pot, pour in water, insert trivet stand, place jars on it, and shut the instant pot with its lid in the sealed position.
4. Press the "Manual" button, press "+/-" to set the cooking time to 5 minutes, and cook at a high-pressure setting; when the pressure builds in the pot, the cooking timer will start.
5. When the instant pot buzzes, press the 'keep warm' button, do a quick pressure release and open the lid.
6. Carefully remove the jars, let them cool at room temperature for 15 minutes or more until they can be comfortably picked up.
7. Then transfer the custard jars into the refrigerator for a minimum of 4 hours and cool completely.
8. When ready to serve, shake the jars a few times to mix all the ingredients and then serve.

## Nutrition

- Calories: 262
- Fat: 24 g.
- Protein: 5 g.
- Net carbs: 3 g.
- Fiber: 3 g.

# 137.    Chocolate Avocado Ice Cream

**Preparation time:** 12 hours and 10 minutes

**Cooking time:** 0

**Servings:** 6

## Ingredients

- 2 large organic avocados, pitted
- ½ c. Erythritol, powdered
- ½ c. cocoa powder, organic and unsweetened
- 25 drops of liquid Stevia
- 2 tsps. vanilla extract, unsweetened
- 1 c. coconut milk, full-fat: and unsweetened
- ½ c. heavy whipping cream, full-fat
- 6 squares of chocolate, unsweetened and chopped

## Directions

1. Scoop out the flesh from each avocado, place it in a bowl and add vanilla, milk, and cream and blend using an immersion blender until smooth and creamy.
2. Add the remaining ingredients except for chocolate and mix until well combined and smooth.
3. Fold in chopped chocolate and let the mixture chill in the refrigerator for 8–12 hours or until cooled.

4. When ready to serve, let ice cream stand for 30 minutes at room temperature, then process it using an ice cream machine as per manufacturer instruction.
5. Serve immediately.

## Nutrition

- Calories: 216.7
- Fat: 19.4 g.
- Protein: 3.8 g.
- Net carbs: 3.7 g.
- Fiber: 7.4 g.

# 138.    Key Lime Curd

**Preparation time:** 4 hours and 30 minutes

**Cooking time:** 10 minutes

**Servings:** 3

## Ingredients

- 3 oz. butter, unsalted
- 1 c. Erythritol sweetener
- 2 eggs
- 2 egg yolks
- ⅔ c. key lime juice
- 2 tsps. key lime zest
- 1 ½ c. water

## Directions

1. Place butter in a food processor, add sugar, blend for 2 minutes, then add eggs and yolks and continue blending for 1 minute.
2. Add lime juice, blend until combined and a smooth curd comes together, and then pour the mixture evenly into three half-pint mason jars.

3. Switch on the instant pot, pour in water, insert a trivet stand, place mason jars on it and shut the instant pot with its lid in the sealed position.
4. Press the "Manual" button, press "+/-" to set the cooking time to 10 minutes, and cook at a high-pressure setting; when the pressure builds in the pot, the cooking timer will start.
5. When the instant pot buzzes, press the 'keep warm' button, release pressure naturally for 10 minutes, then do a quick pressure release and open the lid.
6. Remove jars from the instant pot, open them, add lime zest, stir until combined, and then close the jars with their lids again.
7. Let the jars cool at room temperature for 20 minutes, then place them in the refrigerator for 4 hours or more until chilled and curd gets thickened.
8. Serve straight away.

## Nutrition

- Calories: 78
- Fat: 4.5 g.
- Protein: 7 g.
- Net carbs: 1 g.
- Fiber: 1 g.

## 139.     Cookie Ice Cream

**Preparation time:** 5 minutes

**Cooking time:** 2 hours

**Servings:** 2

### Ingredients

- Cookie crumbs
- ¾ c. almond flour
- ¼ c. cocoa powder
- ¼ tsp. baking soda
- ¼ c. Erythritol
- ½ tsp. vanilla extract
- 1 ½ tbsp. coconut oil, softened
- 1 large egg, room temperature
- Pinch of salt

### Ice cream:

- 1 ½ c. whipping cream
- 1 tbsp. vanilla extract
- ½ c. Erythritol
- ½ c. almond milk, unsweetened

## Directions

1. Preheat the oven at 300°F. and layer a 9-inch baking pan with wax paper.
2. Whisk almond flour with baking soda, cocoa powder, salt, and Erythritol in a medium bowl.
3. Stir in coconut oil and vanilla extract then mix well until crumbly.
4. Whisk in egg and mix well to form the dough.
5. Spread this dough in the prepared pan and bake for 20 minutes in the preheated oven.
6. Allow the crust to cool then crush it finely into crumbles.
7. Beat cream in a large bowl with a hand mixer until it forms a stiff peak.
8. Stir in Erythritol and vanilla extract then mix well until fully incorporated.
9. Pour in milk and blend well until smooth.
10. Add this mixture to an ice cream machine and churn as per the machine's instructions.
11. Add cookie crumbles to the ice cream in the machine and churn again.
12. Place the ice cream in a sealable container and freeze for 2 hours.
13. Scoop out the ice cream and serve.
14. Enjoy.

## Nutrition

- Calories: 214
- Total fat: 19 g.
- Saturated fat: 5.8 g.
- Cholesterol: 15 mg.
- Sodium: 123 mg.
- Total carbs: 6.5 g.
- Sugar: 1.9 g.
- Fiber: 2.1 g.
- Protein: 6.5 g.

# 140. Cream Cheese Chocolate Mousse

**Preparation time:** 10 minutes

**Cooking time:** 0

**Servings:** 2

## Ingredients

- 3 oz. (85 g.) cream cheese, softened
- ½ c. heavy cream
- tsp. vanilla extract
- ¼ c. Swerve
- 2 tbsps. cocoa powder
- Pinch salt

## Directions

1. Beat the cream cheese in a large mixing bowl with an electric beater until it makes a fluffy mixture.
2. Switch the beater to low speed, and add the vanilla extract, heavy cream, salt, Swerve, and cocoa powder to beat for 2 minutes until it is completely smooth.
3. Chill in the refrigerator until ready to serve.

## Nutrition

- Calories: 270
- Fat: 26.4 g.
- Total carbs: 6.0 g.
- Fiber: 2.0 g.
- Protein: 4.2 g.

# 141.    Sugar-Free Lemon Bars

**Preparation time:** 15 minutes

**Cooking time:** 45 minutes

**Servings:** 8

## Ingredients

- ½ c. butter, melted
- 1 ¾ c. almond flour, divided
- 3 c. powdered Erythritol, divided
- 2 medium-size lemons
- 3 large eggs

## Directions

1. Prepare the parchment paper and baking tray.
2. Combine butter, 1 c. almond flour, ¼ c. Erythritol, and salt. Stir well.
3. Place the mix on the baking sheet, press a little, and put it into the oven (preheated to 350°F). Cook for about 20 minutes. Then set aside to let it cool.
4. Zest 1 lemon and juice all of the lemons in a bowl.
5. Add the eggs, ¾ c. Erythritol, ¾ c. almond flour, and salt. Stir together to create the filling.
6. Pour it on top of the cake and cook for 25 minutes.
7. Cut into small pieces and serve with lemon slices.

## Nutrition

- Carbohydrates: 4 g.
- Fat: 26 g.
- Protein: 8 g.
- Calories: 272

## 142.    Delicious Coffee Ice Cream

**Preparation time:** 10 minutes

**Cooking time:** 5 minutes

**Servings:** 1

### Ingredients

- 6 oz. coconut cream, frozen into ice cubes
- 1 ripe avocado, diced and frozen
- ½ c. coffee expresso
- 2 tbsps. sweetener
- 1 tsp. vanilla extract
- 1 tbsp. water
- Coffee beans

### Directions

1. Take out the frozen coconut cubes and avocado from the fridge. Slightly melt them for 5–10 minutes.
2. Add the sweetener, coffee expresso, and vanilla extract to the coconut avocado mix and whisk with an immersion blender until it becomes creamy (for about 1 minute). Pour in the water and blend for 30 seconds.
3. Top with coffee beans and enjoy!

### Nutrition

- Carbohydrates: 20.5 g.
- Fat: 61 g.
- Protein: 6.3 g.
- Calories: 596

# 143. Fatty Bombs With Cinnamon and Cardamom

**Preparation time:** 10 minutes

**Cooking time:** 35 minutes

**Servings:** 10

## Ingredients

- ½ c. unsweetened coconut, shredded
- 3 oz. unsalted butter
- ¼ tsp. ground green cinnamon
- ¼ ground cardamom
- ½ tsp. vanilla extract

## Directions

1. Roast the unsweetened coconut (choose medium-high heat) until it begins to turn lightly brown.
2. Combine the room-temperature butter, ½ the shredded coconut, cinnamon, cardamom, and vanilla extract in a separate dish. Cool the mix in the fridge for about 5–10 minutes.
3. Form small balls and cover them with the remaining shredded coconut.
4. Cool the balls in the fridge for about 10–15 minutes.

## Nutrition

- Carbohydrates: 0.4 g.
- Fat: 10 g.
- Protein: 0.4 g.
- Calories: 90

# 144.    Vanilla Berry Meringues

**Preparation time:** 15 minutes

**Cooking time:** 1 hour and 45 minutes

**Servings:** 10

## Ingredients

- 1 tsp. vanilla extract
- 3 tbsps. freeze-dried mixed berries, crushed
- 3 large egg whites, at room temperature
- ⅓ c. Erythritol
- 1 tsp. lemon rind

## Directions

1. In a mixing bowl, stir the egg whites until foamy. Add in vanilla extract, lemon rind, and Erythritol; continue to mix, using an electric mixer until stiff and glossy.
2. Add the crushed berries and mix again until well combined. Use 2 tsps. to spoon the meringue onto parchment-lined cookie sheets.
3. Bake at 220°F. for about 1 hour 45 minutes.

## Nutrition

- Calories: 51
- Fat: 0 g.
- Carbs: 4 g.
- Protein: 12 g.
- Fiber: 0.1 g.

# 145.    Hazelnut Cake Squares

**Preparation time:** 10 minutes

**Cooking time:** 25 minutes

**Servings:** 8

## Ingredients

- 2 c. almond meal
- 3 eggs
- 1 tsp. almond extract
- ¾ c. heavy cream
- A pinch of sea salt
- ½ c. coconut oil
- ½ c. hazelnuts, chopped
- ¾ tsp. baking powder
- 1 c. Erythritol
- ½ tsp. ground cinnamon
- ¼ tsp. ground cardamom

## Directions

1. Set the oven to 365°F. Coat the bottom of your baking pan using parchment paper.
2. Thoroughly combine the almond meal, baking powder, Erythritol, cinnamon, cardamom, and salt.
3. After that, stir in the coconut oil, eggs, almond extract, and heavy cream; whisk until everything is well incorporated.
4. Stir in the chopped hazelnuts. Scrape the batter into the baking pan.
5. Bake in the oven for at least 25 minutes.

## Nutrition

- Calories: 241
- Fat: 23.6 g.
- Carbs: 3.7 g.
- Protein: 5.2 g.
- Fiber:1 g.

# 146. Expresso Pudding Shots

**Preparation time:** 10 minutes + chilling time

**Cooking time:** 0 minutes

**Servings:** 6

## Ingredients

- 2 tsps. butter, softened
- A pinch of grated nutmeg
- 1 tsp. pure vanilla extract
- 4 oz. coconut oil
- 3 tbsps. powdered Erythritol
- 4 oz. coconut milk creamer
- 1 tsp. espresso powder

## Directions

1. Melt the butter and coconut oil in a double boiler over medium-low heat.
2. Add in the remaining ingredients and stir to combine.
3. Pour into silicone molds.

## Nutrition

- Calories: 218
- Fat: 24.7 g.
- Carbs: 1.1 g.
- Protein: 0.4 g.
- Fiber:0.7 g.

# 147. Intermittent Lemon Strawberry Cheesecake

**Preparation time:** 15 minutes

**Cooking time:** 0 minutes

**Servings:** 2

## Ingredients

- 2 pieces large strawberries
- 3 oz. cream cheese, softened
- 2 tsps. lemon extract
- ⅓ c. Swerve sweetener
- ¾ c. heavy whipping cream
- Zest of 1 lemon

## Directions

1. Prepare two 8 oz. mason jars.
2. In a mixing bowl, put the whipping cream, sweetener, and cream cheese. Beat them on a high setting until the texture becomes creamy and smooth.
3. Put the lemon extract. Mix thoroughly.
4. Chop one of the strawberries into small pieces. The other strawberry should be sliced into thin heart-shaped slices.
5. Fill each mason jar halfway with the cream cheese mixture.
6. Make a layer of chopped strawberries on top of the cream cheese mixture in each jar.
7. Fill the rest of each jar with the remaining cream cheese mixture.
8. Top each jar with heart-shaped strawberry slices. Arrange the slices to form a flower pattern.
9. Sprinkle some lemon zest at the center of each flower.
10. Put the fridge to chill. Serve.

## Nutrition

- Calories: 474
- Carbs: 5.7 g.
- Fat: 48.2 g.
- Protein: 4.5 g.
- Fiber: 0.4 g.

# 148.   Intermittent Pound Cake (Vanilla Flavor)

**Preparation time:** 15 minutes

**Cooking time:** 50 minutes

**Servings:** 12

## Ingredients

- 2 c. almond flour
- 1 c. granular Erythritol
- 1 c. sour cream
- ½ c. butter (sliced into small squares)
- 2 oz. cream cheese
- 2 tsps. baking powder
- 1 tsp. vanilla extract
- 4 pieces large eggs

## Directions

1. Preheat the oven to 350°F.
2. Prepare a 9" Bundt cake pan and butter it generously.
3. In a mixing bowl, Put the baking powder and almond flour. Mix thoroughly.
4. In a microwave-safe mixing bowl, Put the sliced butter and cream cheese.
5. Microwave them for 30 seconds. Stir the mixture to combine well.
6. Put the sour cream, vanilla extract, and Erythritol into the melted cream cheese mixture. Mix well.
7. Pour the cheese mixture into the mixing bowl containing the flour mixture. Mix well the batter.
8. Put the eggs into the batter. Mix well.
9. Transfer the batter into the prepared Bundt cake pan. Bake the cake for 50 minutes. Do the toothpick test to make sure that the cake is cooked thoroughly.
10. Take out the cake from the oven. Do not remove it immediately from the Bundt pan. It may crumble during the process. Let the cake cool completely in the Bundt pan for 2 hours or more, even overnight.
11. Take out the cake from the Bundt pan. Cut into 12 slices. Serve.

## Nutrition

- Calories: 249
- Carbs: 23.23 g.

- Fat: 20.67 g.
- Protein: 7.67 g.
- Fiber: 2 g.

# 149.  Intermittent Cacao Butter Blondies

**Preparation time:** 15 minutes

**Cooking time:** 20 minutes

**Servings:** 20

## Ingredients

- 6 tbsps. cacao butter
- 6 tbsps. Erythritol, powdered
- 2 tbsps. unsalted butter (softened, room temperature)
- 1 tsp. baking powder
- 2 pieces large eggs (room temperature)
- ¼ c. almond flour
- 2 ½ tbsps. coconut flour
- 2 tbsps. coconut cream
- 2 tbsps. walnuts, ground
- ½ oz. dark chocolate, chopped
- 1 tsp. vanilla bean seeds
- 1 tsp. vanilla extract
- 1 pinch of Stevia extract
- 1 dash salt

## Directions

1. Preheat the oven to 360°F. Prepare a square baking pan (8") and line it with parchment paper.
2. In a microwave-safe mixing bowl, Put the cacao butter. Microwave it for 90 seconds to melt. Stir the melted butter and make sure that there are no more lumps in it. Microwave again to melt the lumps, if needed. Let it cool completely.
3. Once the melted cacao butter is cooled, mix in the unsalted butter and stir.
4. In another mixing bowl, Put the eggs, vanilla bean seeds, vanilla extract, Erythritol, and salt. Mix them well for 2 minutes using an electric hand mixer.
5. Put the coconut cream into the egg mixture. Mix well.
6. Put the cooled melted cacao butter mixture into the egg mixture. Continue mixing until the consistency gets dense.
7. In another mixing bowl, sift the almond flour, coconut flour, and baking powder. Mix well.
8. Pour the flour mixture into the cream mixture. Mix well.
9. Put the chopped chocolate and ground walnuts. Mix well.

10. Transfer the batter into the lined baking pan. Spread out the batter evenly on the baking pan.
11. Bake the batter for 20 minutes. Do not over-bake it. Do the toothpick test to know that it is the right time to take the blondies out from the oven.
12. Carefully take out the entire batch of blondies from the pan, including the parchment paper. Put it on the rack to cool down.
13. Once completely cooled, cut into 20 blondie squares. It is recommended to leave the blondies overnight on the counter before serving.

## Nutrition

- Calories: 80
- Carbs: 1.6 g.
- Fat: 7.3 g.
- Protein: 2.1 g.
- Fiber: 0.9 g.

## 150. Intermittent Cream Cheese Frosted Carrot Mug Cake

**Preparation time:** 10 minutes

**Cooking time:** 2 minutes

**Servings:** 2

## Ingredients

### For the cake:

- 2 tbsps. almond flour
- 1 tbsp. Erythritol
- 1 tbsp. psyllium husk
- 1 tbsp. butter (melted)
- 1 piece large egg (beaten lightly)
- 1 tsp. cinnamon
- ½ tsp. vanilla extract
- ½ tsp. baking powder
- ½ piece small carrot (grated finely)
- ¼ tsp. ginger, ground
- pinch of salt

### For the frosting:

- 1 tbsp. whipping cream
- ¼ c. cream cheese (room temperature)
- ½ tsp. vanilla extract
- ½ tbsp. Erythritol

## Directions

1. In a food processor, Put all the ingredients for the cake. Blend to combine everything.
2. Pour the blended mixture from the food processor into a microwave-safe mug.
3. Microwave it for 90 seconds on a high setting.
4. Remove the cake from the mug. Set it aside to cool down.
5. Cut the cake into two layers. Set aside.
6. In a mixing bowl, Put the cream cheese, vanilla extract, and Erythritol. Whip them up using an electric hand mixer. Continue whipping until the texture of the mixture becomes soft and creamy.

310

7. Put the whipping cream into the cream cheese mixture. Mix thoroughly for 5 minutes.
8. Get the bottom layer of the cake. Scoop a heaping tbsp. the cream cheese frosting. Spread the frosting on top of the bottom layer of the cake.
9. Get the top layer of the cake. Gently put it on top of the frosted bottom layer of the cake.
10. Spread the rest of the cream cheese frosting on top of the cake and the sides.
11. You can chill the cake before serving, or you can serve it right away. Cut the cake in half and enjoy.

## Nutrition

- Calories: 229
- Carbs: 20 g.
- Fat: 17.3 g.
- Protein: 6 g.
- Fiber: 15.9 g.

# 151. Intermittent Avocado Brownies

**Preparation time:** 10 minutes

**Cooking time:** 30 minutes

**Servings:** 12

## Ingredients

- 2 pieces of large avocadoes, ripe
- 100 g. Lily's chocolate chips, melted
- 4 tbsps. cocoa powder
- 3 tbsps. refined coconut oil
- ½ tsp. vanilla
- 2 pieces eggs
- 90 g. almond flour, blanched
- ¼ c. Erythritol
- 1 tsp. baking powder
- 1 tsp. Stevia powder
- ¼ tsp. baking soda
- ¼ tsp. salt

## Directions

1. Preheat the oven to 350°F.
2. In a mixing bowl, Put all the ingredients listed under dry ingredients. Whisk to combine well. Set aside.
3. Cut the avocadoes in half. Scoop out the flesh. Weigh the avocadoes. You will need a total of 250 g. avocadoes for this recipe.
4. Put the avocadoes in a food processor. Process the avocadoes until the texture becomes smooth.
5. Put the rest of the ingredients into the food processor one at a time. Process for a few seconds after each ingredient is added into the avocado mixture.
6. Put the flour mixture into the food processor. Process until everything is well combined.
7. Line a baking dish (12" x 8") with parchment paper. Transfer the avocado batter into the baking dish. Spread the batter evenly on the surface of the baking dish.
8. Bake the batter for 30 minutes. Do the toothpick test to know if the brownie is done. The top surface of the brownie should be soft to the touch.
9. Take the brownie out from the oven. Set it aside to cool down. Cut the brownie into 12 square pieces.

## Nutrition

- Calories: 155
- Carbs: 9.78 g.
- Fat: 14.05 g.
- Protein: 4.02 g.
- Fiber: 6.98 g.

# 152.    Easy Almond Macaroons

**Preparation time:** 15 minutes

**Cooking time:** 8 minutes

**Servings:** 10

## Ingredients

- 3 egg whites
- ½ c. unsweetened shredded coconut
- ¼ c. almond flour
- 2 tbsps. Stevia blend
- 1 tbsp. melted coconut oil
- 1 tbsp. pure vanilla extract
- ½ tsp. pure almond extract
- Pinch of salt

## Directions

1. Stick a medium-sized glass bowl in the freezer and lay a piece of parchment paper on a baking sheet. Preheat the oven to 400°F.
2. Mix flour, shredded coconut, and sugar in another bowl.
3. Mix vanilla and coconut oil in a third bowl.
4. Blend into the flour bowl.
5. Take out the freezer bowl and whisk egg whites vigorously until they get stiff peaks.
6. Slowly mix fluffed egg whites into the flour bowl until just incorporated.
7. With a spoon, lay 10 round blobs of macaroon "batter" on your prepared baking sheet.
8. Bake for 8 minutes, or until the macaroons begin to turn golden.
9. Take out of the oven and cool before enjoying!

## Nutrition

- Calories: 59
- Protein: 1 g.
- Carbs: 2 g.
- Fat: 6 g.
- Fiber: 0 g.

## 153.    Easy Peanut Butter Cups

**Preparation time:** 10 minutes

**Cooking time:** 1 hour 35 minutes

**Servings:** 12 **Servings:**

### Ingredients

- ½ c. peanut butter
- ¼ c. butter
- 3 oz. cacao butter, chopped
- ⅓ c. powdered swerve sweetener
- ½ tsp. vanilla extract
- 4 oz. sugar-free dark chocolate

### Direction

1. Line a muffin tin with parchment paper or c. cake liners.
2. Using low heat, melt the peanut butter, butter, and cacao butter in a saucepan. Stir them until completely combined.
3. Add the vanilla and sweetener until there are no more lumps.
4. Carefully place the mixture in the muffin c.
5. Refrigerate it until firm
6. Put the chocolate in a bowl and set the bowl in boiling water. This is done to avoid direct contact with the heat. Stir the chocolate until completely melted.
7. Take the muffin out of the fridge and drizzle in the chocolate on top. Put it back again in the fridge to firm it up. This should take 15 minutes to finish.
8. Store and serve when needed.

### Nutrition

- Calories: 200
- Fat: 19 g.
- Carbohydrates: 6 g.
- Protein: 2.9 g.
- Fiber: 3.6 g.

## 154.    Raspberry Mousse

**Preparation time:** 10 minutes

**Cooking time:** 4 hours

**Servings:** 8

### Ingredients

- 3 oz. fresh raspberry
- 2 c. heavy whipping cream
- 2 oz. pecans, chopped
- ¼ tsp. vanilla extract
- ½ lemon, the zest

### Directions

1. Pour the whipping cream into the dish and blend until it becomes soft.
2. Put the lemon zest and vanilla into the dish and mix thoroughly.
3. Put the raspberries and nuts into the cream mix and stir well.
4. Cover the dish with plastic wrap and put it in the fridge for 3 hours.
5. Top with raspberries and serve.

### Nutrition

- Carbohydrates: 3 g.
- Fat: 26 g.
- Protein: 2 g.
- Calories: 255

# 155. Chocolate Spread With Hazelnuts

**Preparation time:** 5 minutes

**Cooking time:** 5 minutes

**Servings:** 6

## Ingredients

- 2 tbsps. cacao powder
- 5 oz. hazelnuts, roasted and without shells
- 1 oz. unsalted butter
- ¼ c. coconut oil

## Directions

1. Whisk all the spread ingredients with a blender for as long as you want.
2. Remember, the longer you blend, the smoother your spread.

## Nutrition

- Carbohydrates:2 g.
- Fat: 28 g.
- Protein: 4 g.
- Calories: 271

# 156. Chocolate Peanut Fudge

**Preparation time:** 10 minutes

**Cooking time:** 35 minutes

**Servings:** 12

## Ingredients

- 3 ½ oz. (99 g.) dark chocolate with a minimum of 80% cocoa solids
- 4 tbsps. butter
- 1 pinch salt
- ¼ c. peanut butter
- ½ tsp. vanilla extract
- 1 tsp. ground cinnamon
- 1 ½ oz. (43 g.) salted peanuts, finely chopped

## Directions

1. Mix the chocolate with butter in a microwave-safe bowl, and heat in the microwave the oven or a double boiler to melt.
2. When the chocolate is melted, stir well until it is smooth, and leave the mixture to cool.
3. Mix well and add the remaining ingredients except for nuts, then stir to combine.
4. Transfer this chocolate batter to a greased baking pan lined with parchment paper.
5. Top the batter with peanuts and chill in the refrigerator for 2 hours until firm.
6. Remove from the refrigerator and cut into squares to serve.

## Nutrition

- Calories: 124
- Fat: 10.6 g.
- Total carbs: 5.9 g.
- Fiber: 1.6 g.
- Protein: 2.9 g.

# 157.    Spicy Almond Fat Bombs

**Preparation time:** 10 minutes

**Cooking time:** 4 minutes

**Servings:** 3

## Ingredients

- ¾ c. coconut oil
- ¼ c. almond butter
- ¼ c. cocoa powder
- 3 drops liquid Stevia
- ⅛ tsp. chili powder

## Directions

1. Line a muffin pan with 12 paper liners. Keep aside.
2. Heat the oil in a small saucepan over low heat, then add the almond butter, cocoa powder, Stevia, and chili powder. Stir to combine well.
3. Divide the mixture evenly among the muffin c. and keep the muffin pan in the refrigerator for 15 minutes, or until the bombs are set and firm.
4. Serve immediately or refrigerate to chill until ready to serve.

## Nutrition

- Calories: 160
- Fat: 16.8 g.
- Total carbs: 2.0 g.
- Fiber: 1.2 g.
- Protein: 1.5 g.

# 158.   Chocolate Granola Bars

**Preparation time:** 10 minutes

**Cooking time:** 20 minutes

**Servings:** 20

## Ingredients

- 3 oz. (85 g.) almonds
- 3 oz. (85 g.) walnuts
- 2 oz. (57 g.) sesame seeds
- 2 oz. (57 g.) pumpkin seeds
- 1 oz. (28 g.) flaxseed
- 2 oz. (57 g.) unsweetened coconut, shredded
- 2 oz. (57 g.) dark chocolate with a minimum of 70% cocoa solids
- 6 tbsps. coconut oil
- 4 tbsps. tahini
- 1 tsp. vanilla extract
- 2 tsps. ground cinnamon
- 1 pinch sea salt
- 2 eggs

## Directions

1. Preheat the oven to 350°F (180°C).
2. Except for dark chocolate, process all the ingredients for granola in a food processor until they make a coarse and crumbly mixture.
3. Spread the granola mixture into a greased baking dish lined with parchment paper.
4. Bake the granola for 15–20 minutes in the oven until the cake turns golden brown.
5. Once baked, allow it to cool for 5 minutes, then remove from the baking dish.
6. Cut the granola cake into 24 bars using a sharp knife on a clean work surface. Set aside.
7. Melt the chocolate by heating in a double boiler or the microwave. Let it cool for 5 minutes.
8. Serve the granola bars with the melted chocolate for dipping.

## Nutrition

- Calories: 141
- Fat: 17.2 g.
- Total carbs: 7.0 g.

- Fiber: 3.2 g.
- Protein: 4.7 g.

# 159.    Intermittent Lava Cake

**Preparation time:** 15 minutes

**Cooking time:** 10 minutes

**Servings:** 6

## Ingredients

- 1 tbsp. melted butter, for greasing the ramekins
- 2 oz. (57 g.) dark chocolate with a minimum of 70% cocoa solids
- 2 oz. (57 g.) butter
- ¼ tsp. vanilla extract
- 4 eggs

## Directions

1. Preheat the oven to 400°F (205°C) and lightly grease 4–6 small ramekins with 1 tbsp. melted butter.
2. Cut the chocolate into small pieces on your cutting board. Add the chocolate and butter to a double boiler, and heat until they are melted. Mix well.
3. Add the vanilla to the chocolate mixture, then allow the mixture to cool.
4. Beat all the eggs in a mixing bowl for 3 minutes until fluffy, then add the chocolate mixture. Stir to combine.
5. Divide the mixture among the greased ramekins. Bake all the ramekins in the preheated oven for 5 minutes.
6. Remove from the oven and cool for 5 minutes before enjoying.

## Nutrition

- Calories: 197
- Fat: 17.8 g.
- Total carbs: 4.9 g.
- Fiber: 1.0 g.
- Protein: 5.4 g.

# 160.    Coco Avocado Truffles

**Preparation time:** 35 minutes

**Cooking time:**

**Servings:** 20

## Ingredients

- 1 ripe avocado, chopped
- ½ tsp. vanilla extract
- ½ lime zest
- 1 pinch salt
- 5 oz. (142 g.) dark chocolate with a minimum of 80% cocoa solids, finely chopped
- 1 tbsp. coconut oil
- 1 tbsp. unsweetened cocoa powder

## Directions

1. In a bowl, thoroughly mix the avocado flesh with vanilla extract with an electric hand mixer until it forms a smooth mixture.
2. Add the lime zest and a pinch of salt, then mix well. Set aside.
3. Mix and melt the chocolate with coconut oil in a double broiler or by heating in the microwave. Add the chocolate mixture to the avocado mash. Blend well until a smooth batter forms. Refrigerate this batter for 30 minutes until firm.
4. Scoop portions of the batter (about 2 tsps. in size) and shape into small truffle balls with your hands, then roll each truffle ball in the cocoa powder. Serve immediately.

## Nutrition

- Calories: 61
- Fat: 5.2 g.
- Total carbs: 4.3 g.
- Fiber: 1.6 g.
- Protein: 0.8 g.

# 161.    Pumpkin Spice Fat Bombs

**Preparation time:** 10 minutes + 1 hour freezing

**Cooking time:** 0 minutes

**Servings:** 16

## Ingredients

- ½ c. butter, at room temperature
- ½ c. cream cheese, at room temperature
- ⅓ c. pure pumpkin purée
- 3 tbsps. chopped almonds
- 4 drops liquid Stevia
- ½ tsp. ground cinnamon
- ¼ tsp. ground nutmeg

## Directions

1. Line an 8x8-inch pan with parchment paper and set it aside.
2. In a small bowl, whisk together the butter and cream cheese until very smooth.
3. Add the pumpkin purée and whisk until blended. Stir in the almonds, Stevia, cinnamon, and nutmeg. Spoon the pumpkin mixture into the pan.
4. Use a spatula to spread it equally in the pan, then place it in the freezer for about 1 hour.
5. Cut into 16 pieces and store the fat bombs in a tightly sealed container in the freezer until ready to serve.

## Nutrition

- Calories: 87
- Fat: 9 g.
- Protein: 1 g.
- Carbs: 1 g.
- Fiber: 0 g.
- Net carbs: 1 g.

# 162.    Creamy Banana Fat Bombs

**Preparation time:** 10 minutes + 1 hour chilling

**Cooking time:** 0 minutes

**Servings:** 4

## Ingredients

- 1 ¼ c. cream cheese, at room temperature
- ¾ c. heavy, whipping, cream
- 1 tbsp. pure banana extract
- 6 drops liquid Stevia

## Directions

1. Line a baking sheet using parchment paper then set aside.
2. In a medium bowl, beat together the cream cheese, heavy cream, banana extract, and Stevia until smooth and very thick, about 5 minutes.
3. Gently spoon the mixture onto the baking sheet in mounds, leaving some space between each mound, and place the baking sheet in the refrigerator until firm, about 1 hour.

## Nutrition

- Calories: 134
- Fat: 12 g.
- Protein: 3 g.
- Carbs: 1 g.
- Fiber: 0 g.
- Net carbs: 1 g.

## 163.     Quick and Simple Brownie

**Preparation time:** 20 minutes

**Cooking time:** 5 minutes

**Servings:** 2

### Ingredients

- 3 tbsps. chocolate chips
- 1 tbsp. unsweetened cacao powder
- 2 tbsps. salted butter
- 2¼ tbsp. powdered sugar

### Directions

1. Combine 2 tbsps. chocolate chips and butter, melt them in a microwave for 10–15 minutes. Add the remaining chocolate chips, stir and make a sauce.
2. Add the cacao powder and powdered sugar to the sauce and whisk well until you have a dough.
3. Place the dough on a baking sheet, form the Brownie.
4. Put your Brownie into the oven (preheated to 350°F).
5. Bake for 5 minutes.

### Nutrition

- Carbohydrates: 9 g.
- Fat: 30 g.
- Protein: 13 g.
- Calories: 100

# 164.    Cute Peanut Balls

**Preparation time:** 20 minutes

**Cooking time:** 20 minutes

**Servings:** 18

## Ingredients

- 1 c. salted peanuts, chopped
- 1 c. peanut butter
- 1 c. powdered sweetener
- 8 oz. intermittent chocolate chips

## Directions

1. Combine the chopped peanuts, peanut butter, and sweetener in a separate dish. Stir well and make a dough. Divide it into 18 pieces and form small balls. Put them in the fridge for 10–15 minutes.
2. Use a microwave to melt your chocolate chips.
3. Plunge each ball into the melted chocolate.
4. Return your balls to the fridge. Cool for about 20 minutes.

## Nutrition

- Carbohydrates: 7 g.
- Fat: 17 g.
- Protein: 7 g.
- Calories: 194

# 165.     Chocolate Mug Muffins

**Preparation time:** 5 minutes

**Cooking time:** 2 minutes

**Servings:** 4

## Ingredients

- 4 tbsps. almond flour
- 1 tsp. baking powder
- 4 tbsps. granulated Erythritol
- 2 tbsps. cocoa powder
- ½ tsp. vanilla extract
- 2 pinches salt
- 2 eggs beaten
- 3 tbsps. butter, melted
- 1 tsp. coconut oil, for greasing the mug
- ½ oz. sugar-free dark chocolate, chopped

## Directions

1. Mix the dry ingredients together in a separate bowl. Add the melted butter, beaten eggs, and chocolate to the bowl. Stir thoroughly.
2. Divide your dough into 4 pieces. Put these pieces in the greased mugs and put them in the microwave. Cook for 1–2 minutes (700 watts).
3. Let them cool for 1 minute and serve.

## Nutrition

- Carbohydrates: 2 g.
- Fat: 19 g.
- Protein: 5 g.
- Calories: 208

## 166.  Pumpkin Pecan Ice Cream

**Preparation time:** 4 hours and 5 minutes

**Cooking time:** 0

**Servings:** 4

## Ingredients

- ½ c. cottage cheese
- ½ c. pumpkin puree
- 1 tsp. pumpkin spice
- 2 c. unsweetened coconut milk
- ½ tsp. Xanthan gum
- 3 large egg yolks
- ⅓ c. Erythritol
- 20 drops liquid Stevia
- 1 tsp. maple extract
- ½ c. chopped pecans, toasted
- 2 tbsps. salted butter

## Directions

1. Add butter to a saucepan and place it over low heat until butter turns brown.
2. Whisk the remaining ingredients in a separate bowl using a hand mixer.
3. Churn this mixture in the ice cream mixture as per the machine's instructions.
4. Toss pecans with butter then add them to the ice cream.
5. Churn again then freeze for 4 hours.
6. Enjoy.

## Nutrition

- Calories: 331
- Total fat: 38.5 g.
- Saturated fat: 19.2 g.
- Cholesterol: 141 mg.
- Sodium: 283 mg.
- Total carbs: 9.2 g.
- Sugar: 3 g.
- Fiber: 1 g.
- Protein: 2.1 g.

## 167.    Mocha Ice Cream

**Preparation time:** 2 hours and 5 minutes

**Cooking time:** 0

**Servings:** 2

## Ingredients

- 1 c. coconut milk
- ¼ c. heavy whipping cream
- 2 tbsps. Erythritol
- 15 drops liquid Stevia
- 2 tbsps. unsweetened cocoa powder
- 1 tbsp. instant coffee
- ¼ tsp. Xanthan gum

## Directions

1. Whisk everything except Xanthan gum in a bowl using a hand mixer.
2. Slowly add Xanthan gum and stir well to make a thick mixture.
3. Churn the mixture in an ice cream machine as per the machine's instructions.
4. Freeze it for 2 hours then garnish with mint and instant coffee. Serve.

## Nutrition

- Calories: 267
- Total fat: 44.5 g.
- Saturated fat: 17.4 g.
- Cholesterol: 153 mg.
- Sodium: 217 mg.
- Total carbs: 8.4 g.
- Sugar: 2.3 g.
- Fiber: 1.3 g.
- Protein: 3.1 g.

# 168.    Strawberry Ice Cream

**Preparation time:** 2 hours and 5 minutes

**Cooking time:** 0

**Servings:** 6

## Ingredients

- 1 c. heavy whipping cream
- ⅓ c. Erythritol
- 3 large egg yolks
- ½ tsp. vanilla extract
- ⅛ tsp Xanthan gum
- 1 tbsp. vodka
- 1 c. strawberries, pureed

## Directions

1. Add cream to a pot and place it over low heat and warm it up.
2. Stir in ⅓ c. Erythritol and mix well to dissolve.
3. Beat in egg yolks and continue whisking until fluffy.
4. Stir in vanilla extract and mix well until smooth.
5. Lastly, add ⅛ tsp Xanthan gum and vodka.
6. Mix well then transfer the mixture to an ice cream machine and churn as per the machine's instructions.
7. Freeze it for 1 hour then add pureed strawberries.
8. Churn again and freeze for another 1 hour.
9. Serve.

## Nutrition

- Calories: 259
- Total fat: 34 g.
- Saturated fat: 10.3 g.
- Cholesterol: 112 mg.
- Sodium: 92 mg.
- Total carbs: 8.5 g.
- Sugar: 2 g.
- Fiber: 1.3 g.
- Protein: 7.5 g.

## 169. Intermittent Vanilla Ice Cream

**Preparation time:** 8 hours and 5 minutes

**Cooking time:** 0

**Servings:** 8

### Ingredients

- 15 oz. cans coconut milk
- 2 c. heavy cream
- ¼ c. Swerve confectioner's sweetener
- 1 tsp. pure vanilla extract
- Pinch kosher salt

### Directions

1. Refrigerate coconut milk for 3 hours or overnight and remove the cream from the top while leaving the liquid in the can. Place the cream in a bowl.
2. Beat the coconut cream using a hand mixer until it forms peaks.
3. Stir in vanilla, sweeteners, and whipped cream then beat well until fluffy.
4. Freeze this mixture for 5 hours.
5. Enjoy.

### Nutrition

- Calories: 255
- Total fat: 23.4 g.
- Saturated fat: 11.7 g.
- Cholesterol: 135 mg.
- Sodium: 112 mg.
- Total carbs: 2.5 g.
- Sugar: 12.5 g.
- Fiber: 1 g.
- Protein: 7.9 g.

# 170.    Butter Pecan Ice Cream

**Preparation time:** 5 minutes

**Cooking time:** 5 minutes

**Servings:** 3

## Ingredients

- 1½ c. unsweetened coconut milk
- ¼ c. heavy whipping cream
- 5 tbsps. butter
- ¼ c. crushed pecans
- 25 drops liquid Stevia
- ¼ tsp. Xanthan gum

## Directions

1. Place a pan over medium-low heat and melt butter in it until it turns brown.
2. Mix this butter with chopped pecans, heavy cream, and Stevia in a bowl.
3. Stir in coconut milk then Xanthan gum and mix well until fluffy.
4. Add this mixture to an ice cream machine and churn as per the machine's instructions.
5. Once done, serve.

## Nutrition

- Calories: 251
- Total fat: 24.5 g.
- Saturated fat: 14.7 g.
- Cholesterol: 165 mg.
- Sodium: 142 mg.
- Total carbs: 4.3 g.

# Free Time:

## Appetizers, Snacks, and Coffee Break

**171.** **Pine Nuts & Red Chard**

**Preparation time:** 10 minutes

**Cooking time:** 10 minutes

**Servings:** 4

## Ingredients

- 1 bunch red chard, cut into strips
- tbsps. olive oil
- 1 tbsp. balsamic vinegar
- 1 small yellow onion, chopped
- ¼ c. pine nuts, toasted
- Salt and black pepper to the taste

## Directions

1. Heat up a pan with the oil at medium-high heat, add the onion, stir and cook for 3 minutes.
2. Add the chard, vinegar, salt, and pepper, stir, cook for 7 minutes more, divide between plates, sprinkle the pine nuts and serve as a side dish

## Nutrition

- Calories: 190
- Fat: 2 g.
- Fiber: 6 g.
- Carbs: 8 g.
- Protein: 4g.

## 172. Celery Mix

**Preparation time:** 10 minutes

**Cooking time:** 20 minutes

**Servings:** 4

### Ingredients

- 1 lb. celery, peeled and cubed
- 2 garlic cloves, minced
- Salt and black pepper to the taste
- 1 tbsp. rosemary, chopped
- 1 tbsp. avocado oil

### Directions

1. Heat up a pan with the oil at medium-high heat, add the celery, stir and cook for 5 minutes.
2. Add garlic, salt, pepper, and rosemary, stir, cook for 15 minutes more, divide between plates, and serve as a side dish.

### Nutrition

- Calories: 200
- Fat: 3 g.
- Fiber: 3 g.

- Carbs: 8 g.
- Protein: 9 g.

## 173.     Acorn Squash Puree

**Preparation time:** 10 minutes

**Cooking time:** 20 minutes

**Servings:** 4

## Ingredients

- ½ c. water
- 2 acorn squash, deseeded and halved
- Salt and black pepper to the taste
- 2 tbsps. ghee, melted
- ½ tsp. nutmeg, grated

## Directions

1. Put the squash halves and the water in a pot, bring to a simmer, cook for 20 minutes, drain, scrape squash flesh, transfer to a bowl, add salt, pepper, ghee, and nutmeg, mash well, divide between plates and serve as a side dish.

## Nutrition

- Calories: 182
- Fat: 3 g.
- Fiber: 2 g.
- Carbs: 7 g.

- Protein: 6 g.

# 174.    Squash Wedges

**Preparation time:** 10 minutes

**Cooking time:** 10 minutes

**Servings:** 4

## Ingredients

- 1 lb. butternut squash, cut into medium wedges
- Olive oil for frying
- A pinch of salt and black pepper
- ¼ tsp. baking soda

## Directions

1. Heat a pan with olive oil at medium-high heat, put squash wedges, season with salt, pepper, and the baking soda, cook until they are golden on all sides, drain grease, divide between plates then serve.

## Nutrition

- Calories: 202
- Fat: 5 g.
- Fiber: 5 g.
- Carbs: 7 g.
- Protein: 11 g.

# 175. Turnips Mash

**Preparation time:** 10 minutes

**Cooking time:** 20 minutes

**Servings:** 4

## Ingredients

- 1 lb. turnips, peeled and chopped
- ½ c. veggie stock
- Salt and black pepper to the taste
- 1 yellow onion, chopped
- ¼ c. coconut cream

## Directions

2. In a pot, combine the turnips with stock and onion, stir, bring to a simmer, cook for 20 minutes and blend using an immersion blender.
3. Add salt, pepper, and cream blend again, divide between plates and serve as a side dish.

## Nutrition

- Calories: 201
- Fat: 3 g.
- Fiber: 3 g.
- Carbs: 7 g.
- Protein: 8 g.

# 176.    Cabbage Sauté

**Preparation time:** 5 minutes

**Cooking time:** 10 minutes

**Servings:** 2

## Ingredients

- 3 oz. kale
- 2 oz. green cabbage
- 2 oz. red cabbage
- 1 tbsp. lemon juice
- 2 tbsps. olive oil
- ¼tsp. black pepper
- Salt to taste

## Directions

1. Tear the kale leaves from stems, and cut the cabbage into thin pieces.
2. Take a skillet and heat the oil over low to medium heat. Put everything into a skillet. Pour some lemon juice and season the mixture with some salt and pepper. Stir everything together.
3. Leave the skillet over medium heat and cook the mixture for 5–10 minutes or until you notice it became tender and golden at the edges.

## Nutrition

- Calories: 148
- Total carbs: 6 g.
- Fiber: 2 g.
- Net carbs: 4 g.
- Fat: 14 g.
- Protein: 1 7 g.

# 177.  Creamy Cabbage

**Preparation time:** 5 minutes

**Cooking time:** 10 minutes

**Servings:** 2

## Ingredients

- 1 large cabbage
- 1 garlic clove
- 1 tbsp. butter (or coconut oil)
- 1 oz. vegetable broth (or water)
- 1 ½ oz. heavy cream (or coconut cream)
- Salt to taste

## Directions

1. Cut the cabbage into thin slices and crush the garlic.
2. Take a large skillet and melt the butter over medium-high heat. Add in cabbage and garlic and cook for 3–4 minutes until you notice cabbage got tender.
3. Pour the broth and cream into the skillet and stir everything together. Wait until everything simmers and then cook it for 3–4 more minutes. You will know you are done when the cream is thick, and the cabbage is softer. Serve the meal while it's hot.

## Nutrition

- Calories: 149
- Total carbs: 6 g.
- Fiber: 1 6 g.
- Net carbs: 4 4 g.
- Fat: 14 3 g.

# 178.  Creamy Coleslaw

**Preparation time:** 10 minutes

**Cooking time:** 2 minutes

**Servings:** 2

## Ingredients

- 3 oz. green cabbage
- 1 oz. red cabbage
- 2 oz. cucumber
- black olives
- 1 tbsp. scallions
- 4 tbsps. mayonnaise
- ½ tbsp. lemon juice
- 1 tbsp. dill
- 1 tbsp. parsley
- Salt to taste

## Directions

1. Cut the red and green cabbage, olives, scallions, and cucumber into bite-sized pieces and add them to a bowl. Add some salt.
2. Put the lemon juice and mayo in another bowl. Mince the parsley and dill and combine them in.
3. Mix the wet and dry ingredients so you can prepare coleslaw. You can wait for the mixture to marinate a little bit and leave it aside for an hour or simply serve it right away

## Nutrition

- Calories: 222
- Total carbs: 6 g.
- Fiber: 2 g.
- Net carbs: 4 g.
- Fat: 21 g.
- Protein: 15 g.

## 179. Crispy Bacon and Kale

**Preparation time:** 5 minutes

**Cooking time:** 14 minutes

**Servings:** 2

### Ingredients

- 1 ½ oz. bacon
- 4 oz. kale
- ¼ tsp. black pepper
- Salt to taste

### Directions

1. Take a wide pot (that will be suitable for kale you'll add later), and add bacon. Cook the strips over medium heat until they become crispy. Put them aside.
2. Lower the heat, cut your kale, and place it in the pot. Cook the kale on the bacon grease for 5 minutes or until it becomes wilted. Toss in some pepper and salt.
3. Slice the bacon into smaller pieces and mix it with the kale. Serve it warm!

### Nutrition

- Calories: 116
- Total carbs: 37 g.
- Fiber: 1 2 g.
- Net carbs: 25 g.
- Fat: 77 g.
- Protein: 83 g.

# 180.    Lemon Parsnips Mix

**Preparation time:** 10 minutes

**Cooking time:** 35 minutes

**Servings:** 6

## Ingredients

- 2 lbs. parsnips, cut into medium chunks
- 2 tbsps. lemon peel, grated
- 1 c. veggie stock
- A pinch of salt and black pepper
- 3 tbsps. olive oil
- ¼ c. cilantro, chopped

## Directions

1. Heat up a pan with the oil at medium-high heat, add the parsnips, stir and brown them for 5 minutes.
2. Add lemon peel, stock, salt, pepper, and cilantro, stir, cover the pan, reduce heat to medium and cook for 30 minutes.
3. Divide the mix between, then serve.

## Nutrition

- Calories: 179
- Fat: 4 g.
- Fiber: 4 g.
- Carbs: 6 g.
- Protein: 8 g.

## 181.   Mustard Cabbage

**Preparation time:** 10 minutes

**Cooking time:** 20 minutes

**Servings:** 4

### Ingredients

- 1 onion, sliced
- 1 cabbage head, shredded
- A pinch of salt and black pepper
- 1 c. chicken stock
- 3 tbsps. mustard
- 1 tbsp. olive oil

### Directions

1. Heat up a pan with the oil at medium-high heat, add the onion, stir and cook for 5 minutes.
2. Add the cabbage, salt, pepper, stock, and mustard, stir, cook for 15 minutes, divide between plates and serve as a side dish.

### Nutrition

- Calories: 197
- Fat: 4 g.
- Fiber: 2 g.
- Carbs: 8 g.
- Protein: 5g.

# 182. Radish and Cabbage Mix

**Preparation time:** 40 minutes

**Cooking time:** 15 minutes

**Servings:** 6

## Ingredients

- Salt and black pepper to the taste
- 1 lb. napa cabbage, chopped
- 2 tbsps. veggie stock
- 1 c. radish, chopped
- 3 garlic cloves, minced
- 3 green onion stalks, chopped
- 1 tbsp. coconut aminos
- 3 tbsps. chili flakes
- 1 tbsp. olive oil

## Directions

1. In a bowl, mix the cabbage with salt and black pepper, massage well for 10 minutes, cover, and leave aside for 30 minutes.
2. In another bowl, mix chili flakes with aminos, garlic, onion stalks and oil and whisk well.
3. Heat up a pan with the chili mix over medium-high heat, add the cabbage, stock, and radish, stir, cover, and cook for 15 minutes.
4. Divide between plates then serve.

## Nutrition

- Calories: 200
- Fat: 3 g.
- Fiber: 4 g.
- Carbs: 15 g.
- Protein: 8 g.

## 183.    Paprika Green Cabbage

**Preparation time:** 10 minutes

**Cooking time:** 20 minutes

**Servings:** 4

### Ingredients

- ½ lb. green cabbage, shredded
- Salt and black pepper to the taste
- tbsps. olive oil
- 1 tbsp. parsley, chopped
- 1 c. veggie stock
- ¼ tsp. sweet paprika

### Directions

1. Heat up a pan with the oil at medium-high heat, add cabbage, salt, pepper, paprika, and stock, stir and cook for 20 minutes.
2. Add the parsley, stir, divide between plates and serve as a side dish.

### Nutrition

- Calories: 200
- Fat: 4 g.
- Fiber: 2 g.
- Carbs: 14 g.
- Protein: 5 g.

# 184.    Nori Snack Rolls

**Preparation time:** 5 minutes

**Cooking time:** 10 minutes

**Servings:** 4

## Ingredients

- 2 tbsps. almond, cashew, peanut, or another nut butter
- 2 tbsps. tamari, or soy sauce
- 4 standard nori sheets
- 1 mushroom, sliced
- 1 tbsp. pickled ginger
- ½ c. grated carrots

## Directions

1. Set the oven to 350°F.
2. Combine together the nut butter and tamari until smooth and very thick. Layout a nori sheet, rough side up, the long way.
3. Spread a thin line of the tamari mixture on the far end of the nori sheet, from side to side. Lay the mushroom slices, ginger, and carrots in a line at the other end (the end closest to you).
4. Fold the vegetables inside the nori, rolling toward the tahini mixture, which will seal the roll. Repeat to make 4 rolls.
5. Bring on a baking sheet, then bake for 8–10 minutes, or the rolls are slightly browned and crispy at the ends. Let the rolls cool for a few minutes, then slice each roll into 3 smaller pieces.

## Nutrition

- Calories: 79
- Total fat: 5 g.
- Carbs: 6 g.
- Fiber: 2 g.
- Protein: 4 g.

# 185. Risotto Bites

**Preparation time:** 15 minutes

**Cooking time:** 20 minutes

**Servings:** 12

## Ingredients

- ½ c. bread crumbs
- 1 tsp. paprika
- 1 tsp. chipotle powder or ground cayenne pepper
- 1 ½ c. cold green pea Risotto
- Nonstick cooking spray

## Directions

1. Set the oven to 425°F.
2. Line a baking sheet using parchment paper.
3. On a large plate, put and combine the panko, paprika, and chipotle powder. Set aside.
4. Make the 2 tbsps. the risotto into a ball.
5. Roll in the bread crumbs, then put on the prepared baking sheet.
6. Repeat to make a total of 12 balls.
7. Spray the tops of the risotto bites with nonstick cooking spray then bake for at least 15–20 minutes until it starts to brown.
8. Cool it before storing it in a large airtight container in a single layer.

## Nutrition

- Calories: 100
- Fat: 2 g.
- Protein: 6 g.
- Carbohydrates: 17 g.
- Fiber: 5 g.
- Sugar: 2 g.
- Sodium: 165 mg.

# 186.   Curried Tofu "Egg Salad" Pitas

**Preparation time:** 15 minutes

**Cooking time:** 0 minutes

**Servings:** 4

## Ingredients

- 1 lb. extra-firm tofu, drained and patted dry
- ½ c. vegan mayonnaise, homemade or store-bought
- ¼ c. chopped mango chutney, homemade or store-bought
- 2 tsps. Dijon mustard
- 1 tbsp. hot or mild curry powder
- 1 tsp. salt
- 1⁄8 tsp. ground cayenne
- ¾ c. shredded carrots
- 2 celery ribs, minced
- ¼ c. minced red onion
- 8 small Boston or other soft lettuce leaves
- 4 (7-inch whole-wheat pita bread), halved

## Directions

1. Crumble the tofu then put it in a large bowl. Add the mayonnaise, chutney, mustard, curry powder, salt, and cayenne, and stir well until thoroughly mixed.
2. Add the carrots, celery, and onion and stir to combine. Refrigerate for 30 minutes to allow the flavors to blend.
3. Tuck a lettuce leaf inside each pita pocket, spoon some tofu mixture on top of the lettuce, and serve.

## Nutrition

- Calories: 533
- Protein: 26.13 g.
- Fat: 29.38 g.
- Carbohydrates: 50.62 g.

## 187.    Bacon-Wrapped Mozzarella Sticks

**Preparation time:** 5 minutes

**Cooking time:** 5 minutes

**Servings:** 2

### Ingredients

- 2 slices thick bacon
- 2 Frigo® Cheese Heads String Cheese sticks
- Coconut oil, for frying
- Low-sugar pizza sauce, for dipping

### Directions

1. Warm the oil to 350ºF in a deep fryer.
2. Slice the cheese stick in half. Wrap it with the bacon and close it using the toothpick.
3. Cook the sticks in the hot fryer for 2–3 minutes
4. Drain on a towel and cool. Serve with your sauce.

### Nutrition

- Protein: 7 g.
- Total fat: 9 g.
- Net carbs: 1 g.
- Calories: 103
- Fiber 1 g

## 188. Broiled Bacon Wraps With Dates

**Preparation time:** 10 minutes

**Cooking time:** 15–20 minutes

**Servings:** 6

### Ingredients

- 1 lb. sliced bacon
- 8 oz. pitted dates

### Directions

1. Warm up the oven to reach 425°F.
2. Use a ½ slice of bacon and wrap each of the dates. Close with a toothpick.
3. Put the wraps on a baking tray and bake them for 15–20 minutes. Serve hot.

### Nutrition

- Protein: 19 g.
- Total fat: 10 g.
- Net carbs: 5 g.
- Calories: 203
- Fiber 2 g

## 189.    Chocolate Dipped Candied Bacon

**Preparation time:** 20 minutes

**Cooking time:** 1 hour and 15 minutes

**Servings:** 6

## Ingredients

- 5 tsp. cinnamon
- 2 tbsps. brown sugar alternative—ex. Sukrin Gold
- 16 thin-cut slices Bacon
- 5 oz. cacao butter or coconut oil
- 2 oz. 85% dark chocolate
- 1 tsp. sugar-free maple extract

## Directions

1. Whisk the Sukrin Gold and cinnamon together.
2. Arrange the bacon strips on a parchment paper-lined tray and sprinkle using ½ the mixture.
3. Do the other side with the rest of the seasoning mixture.
4. Set the oven to reach 275°F.
5. Bake until caramelized and crispy (approximately 1 hour and 15 minutes).
6. Heat a skillet to melt the cocoa butter and chocolate.
7. Pour the maple syrup into the mixture and stir well.
8. Set aside until it's room temperature.
9. Arrange the bacon on a platter to cool thoroughly before dipping it into the chocolate.
10. Dip ½ each strip of the bacon into the chocolate.
11. Arrange on a tray for the chocolate to solidify.
12. Either place it in the refrigerator or on the countertop.

## Nutrition

- Protein: 3 g.
- Total fat: 4.1 g.
- Net carbs: 1.1 g.
- Calories: 54
- Fiber 1 g

# 190.    Tropical Coconut Balls

**Preparation time:** 15 minutes

**Cooking time:** 20 minutes

**Servings:** 2

## Ingredients

- 1 c. shredded coconut (unsweetened)
- 6 tbsps. coconut milk (full-fat)
- 2 tbsps. melted coconut oil
- ¼ c. almond flour
- 2 tbsps. lemon juice
- 2 tbsps. ground chia seeds
- Zest of 1 lemon
- 10 drops Stevia (alcohol-free)
- ⅛ tsps. sea salt

## Directions

1. Preheat the oven to 250°F.
2. Place the shredded coconut in a large bowl and pour the coconut milk into it.
3. Add the almond flour, ground chia, sea salt, coconut oil, and lemon zest, and lemon juice to the bowl.
4. Mix everything together until well combined.
5. Take 1 tbsp. the mixture and form a ball out of it. Repeat with the remaining mixture.
6. Line a baking tray using parchment paper and place the small balls on it.
7. If you find the mixture too dry while making the balls, add one tbsp. (extra) of coconut oil to the mixture
8. Bake the coconut balls for 30 minutes and remove them from the oven.
9. Let it cool completely at room temperature.
10. Transfer the balls into another container carefully and refrigerate them for 30 minutes.
11. Serve chilled and enjoy!

## Nutrition

- Calories: 134
- Fat: 13.1 g.
- Protein: 2.2 g.
- Net carb: 1.1 g

- Fiber 1 g

# 191.    Jicama Fries

**Preparation time:** 5 minutes

**Cooking time:** 10 minutes

**Servings:** 2

## Ingredients

- 1 Jicama, sliced into thin strips
- ½ tsp. onion powder
- 2 tbsps. avocado oil
- Cayenne pepper (pinch)
- 1 tsp. paprika
- Sea salt, to taste

## Directions

1. Dry roast the jicama strips in a non-stick frying pan (or you can also grease the pan with a bit of avocado oil)
2. Place the roasted jicama fries into a large bowl and add the onion powder, cayenne pepper, paprika, and sea salt.
3. Drizzle over the avocado oil and toss the contents until the flavors are incorporated well.
4. Serve immediately and enjoy!

## Nutrition

- Calories: 92
- Fat: 7 g.
- Protein: 1 g.
- Net carb: 2 g

## 192.  Ham 'n Cheese Puffs

**Preparation time:** 15 minutes

**Cooking time:** 30 minutes

**Servings:** 8

### Ingredients

- 6 large eggs
- 10 oz. sliced deli ham, diced
- 1½ c. shredded cheddar cheese
- ¾ c. mayonnaise
- ⅓ c. coconut flour
- ⅓ c. coconut oil
- ⅓ tsp. baking powder
- ⅓ tsp. baking soda
- Nonstick cooking spray

### Directions

1. Set the oven to 350°F. Lightly coat rimmed baking sheet using nonstick cooking spray and set aside.
2. In a bowl, put together the eggs, coconut oil, and mayonnaise then mix. Set aside.
3. In a separate bowl, combine the baking soda, baking powder, and coconut flour. Add the dry ingredients to the wet ingredients and mix well until smooth.
4. Fold the ham and cheddar cheese into the mixture and set aside.
5. Cut the dough into 18 small pieces then arrange it on the prepared baking sheet.
6. Bake for 30 minutes, or until the puffs are golden brown and set.
7. Arrange the puffs on a cooling rack and allow them to cool slightly.
8. Keep in a sealed container for up to 5 days. If desired, reheat in the microwave before serving.

### Nutrition

- Calories: 249
- Fat: 20 g.
- Carbs: 3 g.
- Protein: 15 g.

# 193. Walnut Parmesan Bites

**Preparation time:** 10 minutes

**Cooking time:** 10 minutes

**Servings:** 10

## Ingredients

- 6 oz. freshly grated Parmesan cheese
- 2 tbsps. chopped walnuts
- 1 tbsp. unsalted butter
- ½ tbsp. chopped fresh thyme

## Directions

1. Set the oven to 350°F. Line two large rimmed baking sheets with baking paper and set them aside.
2. In a food processor, combine the Parmesan cheese and butter. Blend until combined.
3. Pour in the walnuts and pulse until crushed and combined with the mixture.
4. Using a tbsp. scoop the mixture onto the prepared baking sheets, then top with chopped thyme.
5. Bake for at least 8 minutes, or until golden brown.
6. Transfer to a cooling rack and let sit for about 30 minutes. Serve and enjoy!

## Nutrition

- Calories: 80
- Fat: 3 g.
- Carbs: 7 g.
- Protein: 7 g.

## 194.   **Black Sesame Wonton Chips**

**Preparation time:** 5 minutes

**Cooking time:** 5 minutes

**Servings:** 24

## Ingredients

- 12 vegan Wonton wrappers
- Toasted sesame oil
- 1/3 c. black sesame seeds
- Salt

## Directions

1. Preheat the oven to 450°F. Lightly grease with oil on a baking sheet and set aside. Cut the wonton wrappers in half crosswise, brush them with sesame oil, and arrange them in a single layer on the prepared baking sheet.
2. Sprinkle wonton wrappers with the sesame seeds and salt to taste, and bake until crisp and golden brown, 5–7 minutes. Cool completely before serving.

## Nutrition

- Calories: 89
- Protein: 3.11 g.
- Fat: 4.32 g.
- Carbohydrates: 10 g

## 195.    Tamari Toasted Almonds

**Preparation time:** 2 minutes

**Cooking time:** 8 minutes

**Servings:** 4

## Ingredients

- ½ c. raw almonds, or sunflower seeds
- 2 tbsps. tamari, or soy sauce
- 1 tsp. toasted sesame oil

## Directions

1. Heat a dry skillet to medium-high heat, then add the almonds, stirring very frequently to keep them from burning. Once the almonds are toasted, 7–8 minutes for almonds, or 3–4 minutes for sunflower seeds, pour the tamari and sesame oil into the hot skillet and stir to coat.
2. You can turn off the heat, and as the almonds cool, the tamari mixture will stick to and dry on the nuts.

## Nutrition

- Calories: 89
- Total fat: 8 g.
- Carbs: 3 g.
- Fiber: 2 g.
- Protein: 4 g.

# 196. Avocado and Tempeh Bacon Wraps

**Preparation time:** 10 minutes

**Cooking time:** 8 minutes

**Servings:** 4

## Ingredients

- 2 tbsps. olive oil
- 8 oz. tempeh bacon, homemade or store-bought
- 4 (10-inch) soft flour tortillas or lavash flatbread
- ¼ c. vegan mayonnaise, homemade or store-bought
- 4 large lettuce leaves
- 2 ripe Hass avocados, pitted, peeled, and cut into ¼-inch slices
- 1 large ripe tomato, cut into ¼-inch slices

## Directions

1. In a huge skillet, warm the oil to medium heat temperature. Put the tempeh bacon and cook until browned on both sides, about 8 minutes. Remove from the heat and set aside.
2. Place 1 tortilla on a work surface. Spread with some of the mayonnaise and one-fourth of the lettuce and tomatoes.
3. Peel and pit then thinly slice the avocado and place the slices on top of the tomato. Add the reserved tempeh bacon and roll up tightly. Repeat with the remaining ingredients and serve.

## Nutrition

- Calories: 788
- Protein: 28.25 g.
- Fat: 52.02 g.
- Carbohydrates: 62.36 g

# 197.    Tempeh-Pimiento Cheese Ball

**Preparation time:** 5 minutes

**Cooking time:** 30 minutes

**Servings:** 8

## Ingredients

- 8 oz. tempeh, cut into ½-inch
- 1 (2 oz.) jar of chopped pimientos, drained
- ¼ c. nutritional yeast
- ¼ c. vegan mayonnaise, homemade or store-bought
- 2 tbsps. soy sauce
- ¾ c. chopped pecans

## Directions

1. In a medium saucepan with simmering water, cook the tempeh for at least 30 minutes. Set aside to cool. In a food processor, combine the cooled tempeh, pimientos, nutritional yeast, mayo, and soy sauce. Process until smooth.
2. Transfer the tempeh mixture to a bowl and refrigerate until firm and chilled, at least 2 hours or overnight.
3. In a dry skillet, toast the pecans at medium heat until lightly toasted, about 5 minutes. Set aside to cool.
4. Form the tempeh mixture into a ball, and roll it in the pecans, pressing the nuts lightly into the tempeh mixture, so they stick. Place in the fridge for at least 1 hour before serving.

## Nutrition

- Calories: 304
- Protein: 17.59 g.
- Fat: 21.09 g.
- Carbohydrates: 13.26 g.

## 198.   **Bulletproof Coffee**

**Preparation time:** 5 minutes

**Cooking time:** 0 minutes

**Servings:** 1

### Ingredients

- 2 tbsps. MCT oil powder
- 2 tbsps. ghee/butter
- 1.5 c. hot coffee

### Directions

1. Empty the hot coffee into your blender.
2. Pour in the powder and butter. Blend until frothy.
3. Enjoy in a large mug.

### Nutrition

- Protein: 1 g.
- Total fat: 51 g.
- Net carbs: 0 g.
- Calories: 463

## 199.    Peanut Butter Caramel Milkshake

**Preparation time:** 5 minutes

**Cooking time:** 0 minutes

**Servings:** 1

## Ingredients

- 2 tbsps. natural peanut butter
- tbsp. MCT oil
- 25 tsps. Xanthan gum
- 1 c. coconut milk
- 7 Ice cubes
- Tbsps. sugar-free salted caramel syrup

## Directions

1. Combine each of the components in a blender.
2. Mix thoroughly and serve in a chilled mug.

## Nutrition

- Protein: 8 g.
- Total fat: 35 g.
- Net carbs: 5 g.
- Calories: 365

# 200. Chocolate Shakes

**Preparation time:** 10 minutes

**Cooking time:** 0 minutes

**Servings:** 2

## Ingredients

- 4 oz. coconut milk
- 75 c. heavy whipping cream
- tbsp. swerve natural sweetener
- 25 tsps. vanilla extract
- tbsps. unsweetened cocoa powder

## Directions

1. Empty the cream into a cold metal bowl. Use your hand mixer and chilled beaters to form stiff peaks.
2. Slowly add the milk into the cream. Add in the rest of the fixings.
3. Stir well and pour into two frosty glasses. Chill in the freezer one hour before serving. Stir several times.

## Nutrition

- Protein: 4 g.
- Total fat: 47 g.
- Net carbs: 7 g.
- Calories: 210

Made in the USA
Las Vegas, NV
10 January 2023

65368235R00203